MW00611688

ALSO BY JOAN NATHAN

My Life in Recipes

King Solomon's Table

Quiches, Kugels, and Couscous: My Search for Jewish Cooking in France

The New American Cooking

The Foods of Israel Today

The Jewish Holiday Baker

Jewish Cooking in America

An American Folklife Cookbook

The Jewish Holiday Kitchen

The Flavor of Jerusalem (with Judy Stacey Goldman)

A Sweet Year

A Sweet Year

JEWISH CELEBRATIONS AND FESTIVE RECIPES
FOR KIDS AND THEIR FAMILIES

Joan Nathan

PHOTOGRAPHS BY
GABRIELA HERMAN

Alfred A. Knopf
New York
2024

THIS IS A BORZOI BOOK PUBLISHED BY ALFRED A. KNOPF

Copyright © 1987, 1995, 2024 by Joan Nathan

Photographs copyright © 2024 by Gabriela Herman

All rights reserved. Published in the United States by Alfred A. Knopf, a division of Penguin Random House LLC, New York, and distributed in Canada by Penguin Random House Canada Limited, Toronto.

www.aaknopf.com

Knopf, Borzoi Books, and the colophon are registered trademarks of Penguin Random House LLC.

A portion of this book was originally published under the title *The Children's Jewish Holiday Kitchen* in 1987, and in a revised edition in 1995.

Passover Chocolate Almond Cake is excerpted from *Zahav* by MICHAEL SOLOMONOV and STEVEN COOK. Copyright © 2015 by MICHAEL SOLOMONOV and STEVEN COOK. Used by permission of Houghton Mifflin Harcourt. All rights reserved.

Library of Congress Cataloging-in-Publication Data
Names: Nathan, Joan, author.
Title: A sweet year : Jewish celebrations and festive recipes for kids and their families / Joan Nathan; photographs by Gabriela Herman.
Description: First edition. | New York : Alfred A. Knopf, 2025. | Includes index. | Audience: Grades 2–3
Identifiers: LCCN 2023049938 | ISBN 9780593801895 (hardcover) | ISBN 9780593801901 (ebook)
Subjects: LCSH: Jewish cooking—Juvenile literature. | Fasts and feasts—Judaism—Juvenile literature. | Holiday cooking—Judaism—Juvenile literature. | Food—Religious aspects—Judaism—Juvenile literature. | LCGFT: Cookbooks.
Classification: LCC TX724 .N383 2025 | DDC 641.5/676—dc23/eng/20240314
LC record available at https://lccn.loc.gov/2023049938

Jacket illustration by Angelina Bambina/Shutterstock
Jacket design by Kelly Blair

Manufactured in China

FOR ALMA AND AVIV,

in the hope that they will carry our food traditions
to the next generation

CONTENTS

Preface ... ix

Kashrut: How do we know what is kosher? ... 3

Sabbath ... 7

Rosh Hashanah ... 45

Yom Kippur ... 63

Sukkot ... 79

Hanukkah ... 101

Tu B'Shevat ... 125

Purim ... 139

Passover ... 155

Shavuot ... 177

Acknowledgments ... 201

Index ... 203

PREFACE

In the mid-1980s, when I wrote the first edition of this book, my older daughter, Daniela, was ten years old, Merissa was five, and David was just a toddler. In the afternoons, a group of their friends came to our house in Chevy Chase, Maryland, and later in Washington, D.C., where we cooked the recipes, learning to make challah, pasta with pesto, and even Yemenite chicken soup, all slightly exotic in those days. Now Daniela is the mother of my first grandchildren, twins Aviv and Alma, two kindergartners, who are about the same age as Merissa was when this book was first written as *The Children's Jewish Holiday Kitchen*. Through the years, as my children grew into adults, the book stayed in print; it was updated in 1995. And now I have been asked to update it once again for yet another generation.

During my life, I have written mostly about Jewish food, peeking into kitchens the world over, recording a tale of amazing evolution and adaptation—in this country, in Israel, and wherever I have found Jewish families in my travels. When my family was growing up, I—like so many others—made Moroccan chicken with olives and preserved lemon one day, Tex-Mex fajitas the next, and Chinese stir-fry after that. My children's dishes may have had less bite than they did in homes in the places where the recipes had originated, but our meals were still a far cry from those of my childhood, when each day of the week was assigned a meat-centric dish—meatloaf, lamb chops, chicken, spaghetti and meatballs, liver, and tuna casserole—with traditional Ashkenazi Jewish foods brought out for Friday night and the holidays, even in my assimilated American Jewish home.

In today's multicultural America, much has changed to adapt to different types of diets and a changing world. Hummus, for example, is a household staple, as well known as peanut butter—and rightfully so. Chickpeas, one of the most ancient proteins, are drought resistant and quick-growing; they will be even more important in a future in which we must preserve water and land. My children are so conscious of the food they eat and, for the most part, eat so much less meat than before. They read the ingredients of processed foods, and eat fewer of them.

In the pages that follow, chefs like Ori Menashe, Yotam Ottolenghi, and Mike Solomonov share recipes they make with their own children. I don't think my dad ever cooked, and my late husband, Allan, made only one dish—omelets. But, luckily, it is now common for both parents to share the cooking in their very busy lives.

Fortunately, in my children's lives at home and at school, the dinner table was a constant, binding us together as a family. Judaism provides a joyous ending to each week. Even in very assimilated homes, communal Shabbat dinners and dairy potluck lunches at synagogues provide community for all of us who need it in this fragmented world. I've always loved to open my door to people from many backgrounds, who enrich me with their presence—and their recipes.

I am happy to say that my children try to make time each evening for a shared meal, a refreshing pause when they can catch up with their friends and family. This book is a testimony to that time together. It includes twenty-five new recipes, which we as a family developed and cooked together often. As we traveled over the years, we learned so much and acquired new tastes. Many of these are shared in this new edition: a date-tahini banana milkshake, a rainbow challah, an Australian carrot dip, and a delicious lightly curried and spiced lentil, squash, and carrot soup from my grandchildren's Blossom nursery school in Warsaw, to name a few. Kids still love sweets—like my D.C. neighborhood bakery's Bread Furst Brownies—so the book includes lots of desserts, but what I like in my children's generation is that a sweet dessert is a special treat, not an everyday thing.

This generation is less interested in meat, and more in vegetarian meals with less fat. Even my six-year-old grandchildren are aware of climate change and how it affects what they eat. And they have definite ideas of what they like. As my son, David, told me when I was preparing the 1995 edition of the book, "Mom, kids like plain lasagna, no lumps in their food. They like smooth tomato sauce!" When I talked to him now—thirty-eight years old and a filmmaker—he said, "I'm still a vegetarian for the most part—even more so now. But I'll take the chunks back in my tomato sauce."

Through the years and many cookbooks later, as I travel the country speaking about Jewish food, I have been gratified to discover how many children have learned to cook from these recipes.

Because of the symbolic dishes associated with Judaism, food is a perfect vehicle to introduce children to the many aspects of their religion. They will feel good about helping to prepare the holiday and Sabbath meals. The aims of this book are the same as they were when it was first published:

simply, to have fun making Jewish holiday recipes that the whole family can enjoy; to teach children some of the basics of cooking and our holidays; and, in the process, to explore and explain the meaning and history behind Jewish food. The premise is that cooking will be a cooperative, joyous effort between adults and children. And when children take ownership over their food, they learn to appreciate it all the more.

A Sweet Year is divided into nine holidays, with menus and recipes for each. Feel free to cross over with your meals. An asterisk by the recipe name in a menu means you can find the recipe in this book. And, as I discovered from going through these celebrations with my children, meaning and memories are greatly enhanced when we all participate together in the preparations.

All of the recipes specify the ingredients, equipment, and steps suitable for children to use or do by themselves or with adults or older children; the adults will assign tasks to match the skills of the cooks. And I have given suggestions for menus, but try your own, too. Cooking skills such as separating eggs, using knives, rolling out pie crust, blanching almonds, proofing yeast, and even pitting cherries are explained in the course of the recipes. Learning these basic skills will serve your children well throughout all their days in the kitchen.

Margarine and Crisco seem to be a thing of the past, with vegan spreads, coconut oil, and delicious vegetable and fruit olive oils available to all of us. I will list olive oil and sometimes extra-virgin olive oil for cooking sauces. If you can afford it, I urge you to use small-batch extra-virgin olive oil for your salad dressings. For baking, use vegetable oil. I must confess that I use sprays for baking pans. But instead of spray cans, you can use a simple spray bottle with your own oil inside. Do a taste test with the children. They'll tell you the difference in all these tastes. Do the same with the salts you use. I use fine salt in baking, with coarse salts—kosher, or sometimes Maldon or Jacobsen—for soups and such.

These are foods that children and adults alike will enjoy. I have used real Jewish holiday recipes, some of which have been simplified for children but still satisfy adult tastes. I also sneaked in the culinary traditions we especially like in our family—such as my granola—omitting those that are not child-centered.

The recipes represent a sampling from Israel and many of the countries in the Jewish Diaspora. Israeli food is renowned throughout the world for its light, vegetable-based dishes and staples like tahini, chickpeas, Israeli couscous, and more.

I also include stories, some about the ways grandparents and other ancestors, going back through Europe and the Orient to ancient Israel, may have served the food on their own tables. Still others, like the cupcake menorah for Hanukkah or the matzo pizza, are 100 percent American.

In addition to the recipes themselves, *A Sweet Year* shows how a family can celebrate the holidays and enjoy craft activities such as making challah covers and candlesticks, and includes hints for introducing children to the Torah portion of the week. Tips for making challahs for large or small families are also given.

One last word to the wise parent or older child should be sufficient: Before you begin cooking, fill your sink with warm, sudsy water and bright-colored sponges. Let your children know early on that cleaning up as they go along is part of the activity.

When I first wrote this book, my children treated cookie dough like Play-Doh. Now, I am happy to say, they are great start-from-scratch serious cooks and treat food with respect (most of the time!). They want to learn. Cooking is great for learning math, how to accomplish a task quickly, and how to taste, to touch, and to appreciate the food that grows from the earth and the trees. For me, personally, one of the benefits of cooking with my own children and grandchildren is that it gives us a chance to talk and to relax together. (And how relaxing it is to talk while snipping beans or shelling peas.) I hope you will have as much pleasure cooking from this book with your family as I have had with my own throughout the many decades of my life. Given all the different ways Jews celebrate their religion today, I've tried to make this book as inclusive as I make my own dining-room table. Just as I have organically developed our traditions for friends and family throughout my life, I am sharing them with you so you can happily create your own family traditions.

A Sweet Year

KASHRUT

HOW DO WE KNOW WHAT IS KOSHER?

For three thousand years, Jews have adhered to their dietary laws. These laws were written in the Bible.

"Whatsoever parteth the hoof, and is wholly cloven-footed, and cheweth the cud . . . that may ye eat" (Leviticus 11:3). With the help of illustrated books, magazines, and online searches, let the children discover which meats are permissible for Jews to eat, and why. Beef, veal, lamb, and mutton are a few; any part of a pig is forbidden. But what about a lion? A gerbil? A unicorn? A dinosaur? This exercise can be fun, as well as instructive. Believe it or not, giraffes are kosher (fit to eat)!

As specific as the Bible is about red-meat animals, it is equally vague about fowl. Twenty-four kinds of birds are specifically prohibited in Leviticus 11:13–19: "And these ye shall have in detestation among the fowls; they shall not be eaten, they are a detestable thing: the great vulture, and the bearded vulture, and the osprey; and the kite, and the falcon after its kinds; every raven after its kinds; and the ostrich, and the knight-hawk, and the sea-mew, and the hawk after its kinds; and the little owl, and the cormorant, and the great owl; and the horned owl, and the pelican, and the carrion-vulture; and the stork, and the heron after its kinds, and the hoopoe, and the bat." These are mainly birds of prey. Some permissible poultry that we eat in this country are turkey, goose, duck, and that Friday-night wonder, chicken.

"These may ye eat of all that are in the waters: whatsoever hath fins and scales in the waters, in the seas, and in the rivers, them may ye eat" (Leviticus 11:9). A clean fish must have both fins and scales, and the scales must be detachable from the skin. Bluefish, salmon, cod, scrod, flounder, whitefish, carp, pike, and sole are all allowed, but none of the fish with fins, such as catfish, wolffish, or even monkfish. Some do not eat swordfish, because its scales fall off in adulthood. Shellfish, such as shrimp, lobster, clams, and oysters, lack fins and scales and are scavengers, so they are not kosher. But seahorses? To help your children understand what is kosher, take a look at a book with pictures of different kinds of fish in it.

Before any meat is eaten, the animal must be slaughtered in a kosher manner. A limb torn or cut from a living animal is forbidden. An animal that is not slaughtered, but that dies of itself, is also prohibited. Only select animals, thoroughly tested, are used. What is particularly important to Jews is that for thousands of years so many of them have adhered to this prohibition.

Another Jewish distinction is the way in which animals are slaughtered. The rules for slaughtering spring from ethical principles and are also designed to reject the sacrificial practices of paganism. "If the place which Adonai shall choose to put His name there be too far from thee, then thou shalt kill of thy herd and of thy flock, which Adonai hath given thee, as I have commanded thee, and thou shalt eat within thy gates, after all the desire of thy soul" (Deuteronomy 12:21). All meat animals and birds require *shehitah,* the ritual slaughtering with a very clean, sharp knife. The *shohet* (slaughterer) follows a tradition dating back three thousand years to the meat sacrificed at the Temple in Jerusalem when he says, "Blessed art Thou, O Adonai, Sovereign of the universe, who hast commanded us in the ritual of slaughtering."

The Bible says that one must not eat blood. "Therefore I said unto the children of Israel: No soul of you shall eat blood. . . . Ye shall eat the blood of no manner of flesh . . . ; whosoever eateth it shall be cut off" (Leviticus 17:12, 14). Thus, all the blood is removed by soaking in cold water for half an hour, then, the meat is salted for one hour with coarse kosher rather than fine-grained salt (which would dissolve instead of drawing out the blood). Finally, the salt is shaken off and the meat washed three times, so that no blood remains.

Another dietary law prohibits cooking or eating meat and milk together: "Thou shalt not seethe a kid in its mother's milk" (Deuteronomy 14:21). The purpose of this law was to prevent the ancient Hebrews from following pagan customs of animal sacrifice. It was also a way of assisting digestion. This prohibition requires that two separate sets of utensils must be provided for the preparation, serving, and storing of milk and meat dishes, and the utensils must be washed separately. Observant Jews may have two sinks and two sets of sponges, mixing bowls, and dishes, or two sets of blades and bowls for mixers and food processors. Between a milk dish and a meat meal, one must merely rinse out the mouth or eat a morsel of bread; for this, there is no requirement to wait. Between a meat and a milk meal, however, where digestion is more difficult, Jews wait anywhere from one to six hours.

Neutral or *pareve* foods, such as fish, eggs, and vegetables, may be used with either milk or meat. Some Jews will not eat *pareve* foods outside the home for fear that they may have been cooked in a forbidden fat (lard, or butter during a meat meal).

Many packaged foods are marked with symbols such as "U" or "K" to indicate that a Jewish organization has approved them as kosher. A number of different symbols are used in various parts of the country.

Even if you are not kosher, your children should be made aware of the dietary laws. Visit a kosher butcher and watch the koshering of meat. Go to buy the challah at a Jewish bakery and have someone explain the difference between *pareve* and *milchig* (milk) bakery products. Take a field trip to your local grocery store and have a scavenger hunt, letting the children identify products to see which soups, cereals, etc., are marked with the "U" or "K" and/or the word *pareve* on the packages. They (and you) will be surprised at how universal the markings have become.

SABBATH

Grape Juice 17
Challah 18
Rainbow Challah 23
Hummus 26
Chicken Soup with Matzo Balls 28
Matzo Balls 30
Quick Knishes 31
Chicken Schnitzel Tenders 33
Cheese or Spinach Burekas 34
Shakshuka 36
Golda Meir's Chocolate Chip Cookies 38
Mandelbrot 41

Winter Friday Night Menu

Grape Juice*

Challah*

Chicken Soup with Matzo Balls*

Strips of Red, Green, or Yellow Peppers, Cucumbers, and Carrots

Friday Night Pot Roast

Apple Cake Eden*

Summer Friday Night Menu

Quick Knishes*

Tree of Life Fruitful Salad*

Hummus*

Chicken Schnitzel Tenders*

Mixed Berries

Golda Meir's Chocolate Chip Cookies*

Winter Saturday Lunch Menu

Challah*

Children's Cholent*

Chopped Israeli Salad*

Bread Furst Brownies*

Summer Saturday Lunch Menu

Challah*

Hummus*

Cheese or Spinach Burekas*

Persian Cucumber-Yogurt Salad*

Mandelbrot*

SABBATH

In America today, the way each Jewish family spends the Sabbath is highly personal. In our family, we desperately need to slow down and spend time together. When our children were young, sitting still in the synagogue was difficult for them. Whereas my husband, Allan, would occasionally take the older children, I found it extremely difficult with an infant, so I preferred taking long walks as a family or hanging around the house. When my children were preparing for their Bar and Bat Mitzvahs, we found special meaning in going to synagogue as a family. And now my grandchildren are learning nightly prayers and the joys of Shabbat, which in their very early years during the pandemic took place over video chats. Now they sometimes have picnic Shabbat dinners in Los Angeles before going to synagogue, and attend gatherings with different families to confirm that the Sabbath is a different day.

My family's favorite time of the week is still Friday night, when everything relaxes. I always remember, when I lived in Jerusalem, that frantic rush to prepare for the Sabbath. Mothers breathed a sigh of relief when all the preparations were completed, because then they could rest.

Since the death of my beloved husband, I still rarely go out on Friday night, and often invite other families to dine with me. When the children were small, to engage them in our celebration, they drew a decorated menu before each Sabbath, with stars to show which dishes they had cooked themselves (this also alerted adults to the tenor of the meal and let them know that extravagant compliments would not be out of place!).

We set a special table, usually with a white tablecloth, fresh flowers, white candles, our best china, and a challah, which I would bake myself. Now I try to bake with my grandchildren when we are together. The challah is placed on a silver platter my father brought to this country when he emigrated from Germany. For a challah cover, we alternate between one made by Merissa in school, one stitched by my late mother-in-law, and covers I have picked up while traveling in India, Cuba, and Israel. Everybody has their own kiddush cup; some are filled with white or red wine, others with apple or grape juice.

Standing at the table, although I know it is not politically correct, I follow an old Jewish tradition where the women and young girls cover their eyes before the Sabbath begins, then they light two candles and open their eyes to the Sabbath. Then, together, we all say the blessings over the candles:

Baruch atah Adonai Eloheinu melech ha-olam, asher kidshanu b'mitzvotav ve-tzivanu l'hadlik ner shel Shabbat.

Blessed art Thou, Adonai, our God, Sovereign of the universe, who hast sanctified us by Thy commandments, and commanded us to kindle the Sabbath lights.

When Allan was alive, he said the blessings over the wine and the bread in our family, but now I ask if someone knows the blessings, or we all say them together:

Baruch atah Adonai Eloheinu melech ha-olam, borei p'ri ha-gafen.

Blessed art Thou, Adonai, our God, Sovereign of the universe, who creates the fruit of the vine.

We all sip the wine. Before the blessing over the bread is recited, we all hold the challah or touch someone holding the challah to show the connectedness between what we eat from the earth and our own community, and then we say the blessing over the bread:

Baruch atah Adonai Eloheinu melech ha-olam, ha-motzi lechem min ha-aretz.

Blessed art Thou, Adonai, our God, Sovereign of the universe, who bringest forth bread from the earth.

Then one of the children breaks off pieces of bread to pass to everyone who is at the table. We are essentially rippers, not cutters, for the Sabbath, a custom we learned from my father. For some people, this custom is also symbolic of the special peacefulness of the Sabbath, during which a knife is not used, even to cut bread.

When the children were little, Allan would then spread his hands over the heads of the girls and bless them:

Y'simech Elohim k'Sarah, Rivka, Rahel v'Leah.

May the Sovereign of the universe inspire you to live like Sarah, Rebecca, Rachel, and Leah.

For our son, David, he said,

> ***Y'simecha Elohim k'Ephraim v'hi-Menasheh.***
> *May the Sovereign of the universe inspire you to live like Ephraim and Menasheh.*

Then we kissed each of our children and said,

> ***Shabbat shalom.***

Before we ate, Allan would sometimes tell a story from the week's Torah portion, gearing his short talk to the age of our children, sometimes linking what he had to say to the news of the week. Often he would test them by asking questions from the week before. So many commentaries on the portion of the week are available today online. Some helpful books to consult are: *Living a Jewish Life* by Anita Diamant, *Jewish Literacy* by Rabbi Joseph Telushskin, *How to Raise a Jewish Child: A Practical Handbook for Family Life* by Anita Diamant with Karen Kushner, *To Life!: A Celebration of Jewish Being and Thinking* by Rabbi Harold S. Kushner, and *A Letter in the Scroll: Understanding Our Jewish Identity and Exploring the Legacy of the World's Oldest Religion* by Rabbi Jonathan Sacks.

Occasionally, we sing Hebrew and Yiddish songs. When our children were young, when they finished the main course and sometimes before, they would leave the room to prepare a skit, often from the Bible, which they performed before dessert. Soon I hope my grandchildren will do the same. *L'dor v'dor*—From generation to generation.

Sabbath Cooking Crafts

In order to make your children feel part of the Sabbath ritual, or that of any holiday, let them make their own challah board, challah cover, kiddush cup, and whatever else can be used at the table.

Challah cutting and presentation board

Use any old board that seems the shape you would like for a challah board. Today craft stores sell a variety of wooden "plaques" that are just right for a challah board. Sand the wood. Let the children paint it, or even make handprints in finger paint and shellac it.

Challah cover

Use a piece of cotton or other non-water-repellent fabric. Men's handkerchiefs are a good size. Place water in jars with vegetable skins for color: grapes for purple, onion skins for brown, beets for red, parsley for green. Zap them in the microwave, or boil them until you get the color you wish. The children can then use a paintbrush or medicine droppers to color the cover. This is an especially nice task at Rosh Hashanah or Sukkot, with the different fruits and vegetables of the harvest used as the paints. Rinse the cover in vinegar, which will set the color. More simply, cookie cutters dipped in fabric paint also create a lovely cover.

Shabbat place mats

Let the children paint or color cardboard or durable construction paper. Then cover with clear contact paper or laminate at a nearby store for a lasting mat.

Kiddush cups

Have the children decorate plastic cups with permanent marking pens and write the names of each family member and guest on them. They can then be used as place cards as well, or let the children contribute even more creativity to the occasion by making place cards. I always save them, using them each time the guests come. Yogurt glass cups work well, too.

Candlestick holders

Have the children make the holders out of homemade clay. Mix together four cups flour, one cup salt, and about one and a half cups water to make a stiff dough. Divide the dough into balls the size of Ping-Pong balls. The children can mold them as they wish. Then, while the dough is still soft, they insert the candle they will use to make a hole. Let air dry.

GRAPE JUICE

Makes about 8 cups grape juice

INGREDIENTS

6 cups Concord, Thompson, or Ribier grapes

½ to 1 cup sugar, or to taste (see procedure)

EQUIPMENT

Measuring cups

2 large pots, 1 with a lid

Potato masher or large spoon for each child

Colander

Serving pitcher

Pearl Sofaer, the late author of the cookbook *From Baghdad to Bombay,* told me that her role as the eldest daughter in a Jewish family in India was to make grape juice fresh each Thursday for the Sabbath meal. When dark grapes were not available, she used dried black raisins that were soaked in water, then boiled. When my family went to Cochin and had Shabbat dinner with one of the few Jews left there, we drank this very "wine" and ate a flattened bread instead of challah with a delicious chicken curry, proving once again that Jewish food is so influenced by the region in which we live.

And yet, wherever you live, the following prayer is said over the wine every Friday night. To children in Israel at the time of the Bible, this meant grape juice—not apple or other fruit juices.

Baruch atah Adonai Eloheinu melech ha-olam, borei p'ri ha-gafen.
Blessed art Thou, Adonai, our God, Sovereign of the universe, who creates the fruit of the vine.

Child: Wash the grapes and remove the stems. Place the grapes and 2 cups of water in a large pot. Cover, and cook over low heat, stirring occasionally, until the fruit is softened, about 20 minutes.

Adult: When the fruit is squeezable, place it in a large colander over an empty pot.

Child: Press the fruit with a potato masher or large spoon to squeeze the juice out. Add ½ cup sugar, stir to dissolve, and taste, adding more sugar as needed to taste. When the juice cools, poor into a pitcher and serve cold.

CHALLAH

Paula or Peshke, as we fondly called my mother-in-law, came to this country from Zamość, a beautiful Renaissance town in Poland. When Daniela and Merissa were little girls, she told them the story of how her mother baked the challah each Friday. During the week, the family bought rye bread and white rolls for breakfast at a local bakery. Bagels were snacks, like pretzels in the afternoon after school. Friday was reserved for the sweet challah.

Before making the braided twists of bread, she would break off a morsel of dough and throw it into the wood-burning stove she had at home in her fourth-floor flat, as a reminder of the burnt offering made at the Temple in Jerusalem long ago. Before the challah is eaten, a prayer is always recited over it. In the Friday-night blessing ritual, this bread symbolizes all food that comes from the earth.

Baruch atah Adonai Eloheinu melech ha-olam, ha-motzi lechem min ha-aretz.

Blessed art Thou, Adonai, our God, Sovereign of the universe, who brings bread from the earth.

Makes 3 loaves

INGREDIENTS

- 2 scant tablespoons or 2 envelopes active dry yeast
- 1 teaspoon sugar
- 4 large eggs
- ½ cup honey or sugar
- ½ cup vegetable oil
- 1 tablespoon fine salt
- 7 to 8 cups unbleached all-purpose flour
- 2 cups raisins (optional)
- Vegetable spray
- Sesame and/or poppy seeds

EQUIPMENT

- Measuring cups
- Measuring spoons
- 2 small bowls
- Spoon
- 2 large bowls
- Fork or wire whisk
- Wooden spoon
- Clean dish towel
- 2 baking sheets
- 9-inch round pan
- Parchment paper
- Pastry brush

Challah Baking Hints

The following recipe makes three loaves. If your family is small and you don't want to use the leftovers for breakfast, experiment with forming the bread into four loaves, which you can freeze for a month of Sabbaths. We make Thursday our challah day. When my children were little, I prepared the dough in the morning, often with them, then let it rise (first in the kitchen and then in the refrigerator). Just before the children came home from school, I removed the dough from the refrigerator. With their friends, they literally punched the dough down and braided the loaves themselves—after all, forming the twists is what they like to do best.

I often made three challah twists and froze one. I sometimes rolled a little of the dough into a rectangle, on top of which I sprinkled either jam or about ½ cup sugar and 1 tablespoon cinnamon, all around. Then I rolled it up jelly-roll-style and baked it with the challahs. I learned this smart pre-Sabbath snack years ago from a book by Isaac Bashevis Singer's older brother, Israel Joshua Singer, *Of a World That Is No More.* "Grandmother was reluctant to give me a piece of the *wyskrobek*—a loaf baked from the last scrapings of [challah] dough and one I coveted above everything else," wrote Singer. My children ate this treat for Friday breakfast or, if they couldn't wait, as a snack when they came home from school on Thursday. And now it is my grandchildren's turn!

Child with Adult: In a small bowl, stir together the yeast, 1½ cups of warm water, and the sugar. Set aside for 10 minutes, and make sure it bubbles (this is called proofing the yeast).

Child: Beat three of the eggs with the honey or sugar in a large bowl with a whisk. Then stir in the oil and salt. Add the yeast mixture, and beat well with a spoon.

Child with Adult: Using 5 cups of the flour, add 1 cup at a time to your mixture, beating well with a wooden spoon after each addition. The dough will be sticky. If you want to use raisins, add them now. You can also use a food processor to blend in the flour.

Child with Adult: Now add 2 more cups of flour, beating well with a wooden spoon until the dough stops clinging to the sides of the bowl. Shake an additional cup of flour onto your work surface, and knead the dough until almost all the flour »

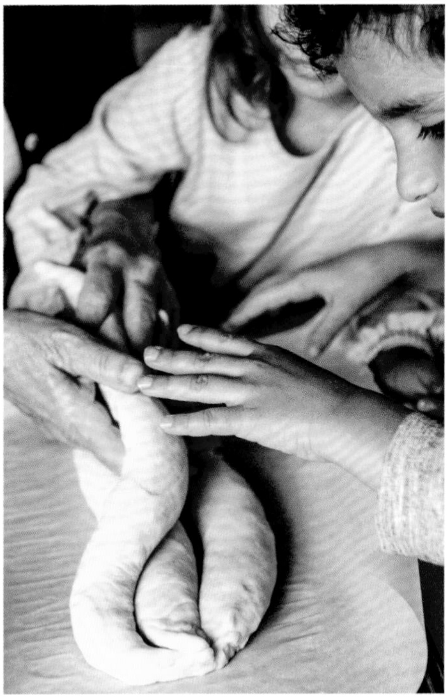
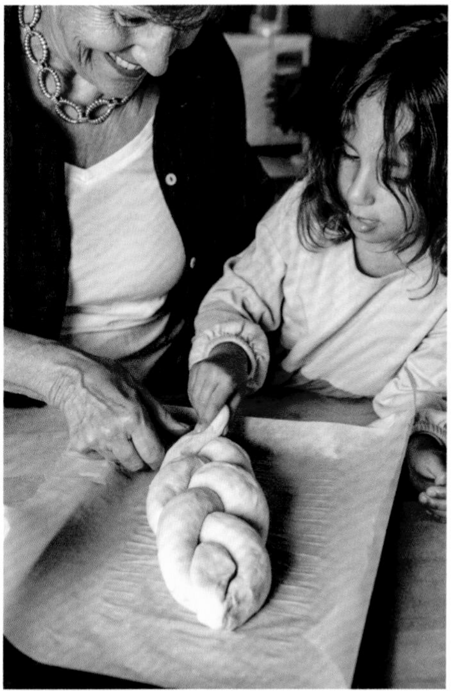
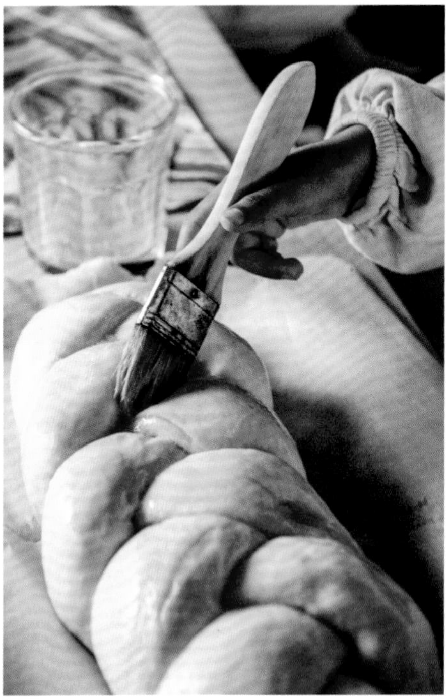

Challah continued »

is absorbed into it. Put the dough in another large bowl greased with vegetable spray. Cover it with a towel and let it rise for 1 to 2 hours, until it has grown to almost twice its size.

Child: When the dough has risen, punch it down. This means just that—hit the dough with your *very* clean fist. And remember, you can always add flour if it is too sticky (but be careful: you don't want an overly dry challah).

Adult: Preheat the oven to 350 degrees Fahrenheit and cover two baking sheets and a 9-inch round baking pan with parchment paper.

Adult: Divide the dough into three equal parts, and divide each part into three again, for braiding.

Child with Adult: To make a braided challah, roll one piece of the dough into three long ropes. Pressing the three ends together, braid the ropes together, as you would braid hair. Then press the ends of the ropes under the loaf and gently lay it on the parchment-lined baking sheet. To make a round challah, take one ball of dough and roll it into a rope about 2 inches in diameter. Coil it from the outside in, letting each circle slightly overlap the one before, gently pressing the top down before transferring to a baking sheet. To make a monkey bread challah, divide the dough into equal rounds about the size of golf balls and set them in a parchment-lined 9-inch baking pan, making sure they barely touch. You should have about twelve balls. »

Challah continued »

Child: Brush the loaves with the remaining egg mixed with a little water in a bowl and let them rise another 20 minutes. Brush the loaves again with the egg wash and sprinkle with sesame and/or poppy seeds.

Adult: Bake for 30 to 35 minutes, rotating the pans halfway through, cooking until the bread is golden and sounds hollow when tapped with a spatula.

Rainbow Challah

To make a rainbow-colored challah, use 6 colors of food coloring and plastic gloves (to avoid dyeing your hands); I recommend AmeriColor natural soft gel paste.

Adult with Child: Mix the yeast with the teaspoon of sugar and 1½ cups of water in a small bowl. Then break three eggs in another small bowl with the honey or sugar, add the oil, and stir everything together. Measure the total liquid, then divide it equally among six small bowls. If possible, use white or clear glass bowls.

Adult with Child: Decide which colors you want to use for the rainbow challah, and mix them into the six bowls until they make the colors you want (hence the light-colored bowls). I use red, orange, yellow, green, blue, and purple, but leave out indigo (you can put a seventh strand with indigo down the center if you want a complete seven-strand rainbow).

Divide the flour into the bowls to make six balls of the same size.

Then make two three-braided long challahs and twist them together to make one large six-color, six-stranded rainbow challah. Proceed as on page 22. You will have to bake the challah for about 35 minutes until it is done. »

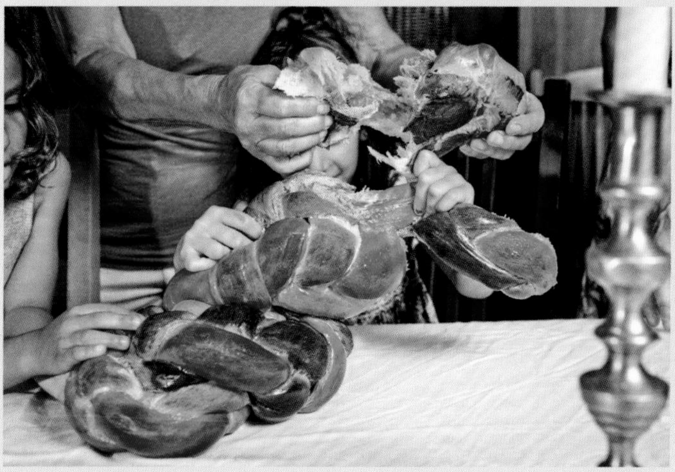

Makes 2 cups

INGREDIENTS

- One 15.5-ounce can chickpeas
- ½ cup tahini (sesame paste)
- 2 cloves garlic, peeled
- Juice of 2 lemons
- 1 teaspoon salt
- 1 teaspoon ground cumin
- 2 tablespoons extra-virgin olive oil
- Paprika, to taste
- Carrot rounds for garnish (optional)
- Olives for garnish (optional)
- Chopped parsley or cilantro for garnish (optional)

EQUIPMENT

- Measuring cup
- Measuring spoons
- Strainer
- Food processor
- Knife
- Mixing bowl
- Wooden spoon
- Plate

HUMMUS

Hummus is probably as popular today the world over as peanut butter and jelly was when I was a little girl. And what better dip to serve with your challah than a homemade version?

Child with Adult: Drain the chickpeas, reserving a few, and put them in the food processor with the tahini and garlic. Purée.

Child: Cut the lemons in half and squeeze them through your fingers. (See the procedure for the Yom Kippur break-the-fast lemonade on page 74.) You want ⅓ cup of juice. Add the juice to the chickpea mixture. Add the salt and cumin to taste. Dip your finger in, taste it, and keep adjusting the spices until the taste is as you like it.

Child: Spread the mixture out on a plate, drizzle the olive oil on top, and sprinkle with paprika and the remaining chickpeas (you can make a design if you like). You can also decorate with cut carrot rounds, olives, chopped parsley, or cilantro—whatever is in your refrigerator.

CHICKEN SOUP WITH MATZO BALLS

Makes about 2 quarts

INGREDIENTS

- One 4-pound hen or roasting chicken, cleaned
- 2 large celery stalks with leaves, chopped
- 2 large carrots, sliced into big chunks
- 1 onion, quartered
- 3 sprigs fresh parsley
- 3 sprigs fresh or 1 teaspoon dried dill
- Salt and pepper, to taste

EQUIPMENT

- Large pot with lid
- Large spoon
- Strainer
- Knife

Jewish chicken soup has achieved international status. Even doctors believe that the soothing properties of the boiled chicken can help bring down the fever from flu. Chicken soup has always been special, because slaughtering and eating a chicken was reserved for special days. Most of the time, the chickens were left to lay eggs. In Europe, during the week, our grandparents ate potato or mushroom-barley soup with a leftover meat bone in it for protein. Chicken soup was reserved for Friday nights or festive occasions. Ask your parents or grandparents if they remember when chickens were bought from the kosher butcher and then cooked with the feet attached (nails cut off, of course!).

Child with Adult: Place the chicken in a pot. Cover with water, about 10 cups.

Adult: Set the pot over high heat to boil, skimming off the bubbling foam as it forms.

Child: Add the celery, carrots, onion, half the parsley and dill, and salt and pepper to taste. Lower the heat, and simmer, half covered, for at least 45 minutes, until the chicken seems done—it will come away easily from the bone.

Adult: Adjust seasonings, letting the children judge the amounts. Pour the soup through a strainer to get a clear broth. Let cool; when the broth has completely cooled, skim off the fat and save it for the matzo balls.

Child: Remove the chicken meat from the bones, using your fingers. Cut the white meat into small chunks, and cut the carrots into rounds. Put them all into the soup. (Cut up some of the meat for dinner, or for a chicken salad. Of course, you're expected to nibble while you work!)

Adult: Reheat the chicken soup before serving and sprinkle each serving with some of the remaining parsley and dill.

MATZO BALLS

Makes about 20

INGREDIENTS

- 4 large eggs, lightly beaten
- ¼ cup chicken fat, or ½ stick vegan spread, melted
- 1 cup matzo meal
- 1 teaspoon salt

EQUIPMENT

- Measuring spoon
- Measuring cups
- Mixing bowl
- Spoon
- Large pot with lid
- Slotted spoon

In our house, matzo balls mean Friday-night dinner or a Jewish holiday. Eyes light up. Maybe it's the soft texture, or the aroma of the chicken soup combined with the mild taste of the matzo dumplings.

Child: Mix together the eggs and the chicken fat or vegan spread. Stir in the matzo meal and salt. Add ¼ cup of warm water. Cover, and refrigerate for at least 1 hour.

Child: Form the matzo dough into balls the size of walnuts.

Child with Adult: In a large pot, bring 12 cups of salted water to a boil. Add the matzo balls, cover, and cook for 20 minutes. (Don't peek! Removing the lid slows down cooking.) Remove them with a slotted spoon, and put them into the simmering chicken broth just a few minutes before serving.

Makes about 18 knishes

INGREDIENTS

- 2 onions, more or less, to taste (amount depends on how much your children like—or dislike—onions)
- 2 tablespoons vegetable oil
- 1¼ pounds russet (baking) potatoes
- Salt, to taste
- 1 pound 1½ ounces prepared puff pastry (2 sheets)*
- 2 large eggs
- ¼ cup chopped fresh parsley
- ½ teaspoon salt, or to taste
- Freshly ground black pepper, to taste
- 1 teaspoon water

EQUIPMENT

- Measuring spoons
- Measuring cup
- Sharp knife
- Frying pan with cover
- Potato peeler
- Cooking pot
- Potato masher
- Rolling pin
- Wax paper or pastry board
- Baking sheet
- Parchment paper
- Pastry brush

* Pepperidge Farm makes a kosher puff pastry.

QUICK KNISHES

In Eastern Europe, children and adults got tired of eating potatoes every day—potato soup; boiled, baked, or mashed potatoes; and even potato skins. One way to avoid that monotony and make a special treat was to wrap the potatoes in a dough. We call these knishes. Some people think the word "knish" comes from the Yiddish *knapen,* to pinch. You'll notice that after you have used your hand to cut the knishes you pinch the top to enclose them. Here's a recipe that my children have loved to make—and, more important, to eat.

Adult: Slice the onions. Slowly cook them in the oil in a skillet, covered, over low heat. Let the onions "sweat" for about 20 minutes, or until they are soft. Then remove the cover and let them fry over medium heat until golden brown. Don't drain them.

Child: Peel the potatoes, and cut them in half. Put them into a large pot filled with cold water, and salt to taste.

Adult: Bring the potatoes to a boil; then turn the heat down, and cook until they're soft, about 20 minutes. Drain them, and let them cool for 5 minutes. Take the prepared puff pastry from the refrigerator, and let it sit at room temperature for about 20 minutes.

Child with Adult: Using a potato masher, mash the potatoes and add one of the eggs and the parsley, and season with the ½ teaspoon salt, and pepper to taste. Add the onions with the oil, and mix well with your hands. Set this mixture aside while you prepare the dough.

Adult: Preheat the oven to 375 degrees and cover the baking sheet with parchment paper. »

Quick Knishes continued »

Child with Adult: Take one sheet of the puff pastry and roll it out with a rolling pin on wax paper or on a pastry board until it's about ⅛ inch thick. Spread half of the filling (about 1½ cups) on approximately a third of the longer side of the dough, leaving a 1-inch border. Hold on to the wax paper, and roll up the dough from the longer side like a jelly roll. Using the side of your hand like a knife, press the roll sharply into 2-inch pieces. Then, cradling the filled pastry in the palm of one hand, twist and pinch the open ends shut. Repeat with the remaining sheet of prepared puff pastry. Place the knishes, flat side down, on the baking sheet, leaving 2-inch spaces between them.

Child: Mix the remaining egg with 1 teaspoon water. Brush the tops of the knishes with the egg wash, and bake them for 25 to 30 minutes, or until they're golden brown.

CHICKEN SCHNITZEL TENDERS

Serves 4 to 6

INGREDIENTS

- 2 chicken breasts, skinned and boned, about six ounces each
- 1 large egg
- 2 tablespoons warm water
- 3 tablespoons vegetable oil
- 1 tablespoon fresh or 1 teaspoon dried oregano
- Salt and freshly ground black pepper, to taste
- 1 cup panko bread crumbs
- 3 tablespoons wheat germ, toasted (optional)

EQUIPMENT

- Measuring spoons
- Measuring cup
- Sharp knife
- Whisk or fork
- 2 soup bowls
- Baking sheet
- Parchment paper

Believe it or not, there is more schnitzel eaten in Israel per capita than in any other country in the world. And, unlike in Europe, where most schnitzel—usually a thin slice of meat pounded, then breaded and fried—is made from veal or pork, the most popular schnitzel in Israel is made from turkey, which in turn gives Israel the distinction of being the highest per capita consumer of turkey in the world.

You can make schnitzel Israeli-style in one slab of meat per portion, but my children, and now my grandchildren, prefer it in small, thicker pieces made from chicken . . . influenced by chicken nuggets, maybe? When my own children were little, I dipped the pieces in corn flakes, but now I use panko bread crumbs. I still add toasted wheat germ to this recipe; it gives it an added crunch, and it's healthy, too!

Adult: Cut the chicken breasts into ½-by-3-inch strips.

Child with Adult: Beat the egg in a wide soup bowl. Then mix in the warm water, oil, oregano, and salt and pepper. Mix the panko and the wheat germ, if using, in a second bowl. Dip the chicken strips into the egg mixture and then the panko-wheat-germ mixture. When you have done them all, place them on a parchment-lined baking sheet, and chill them in the refrigerator for a few hours.

Adult: Heat the oven to 350 degrees. Bake the schnitzel for 30 minutes, or until golden, flipping halfway through.

CHEESE OR SPINACH BUREKAS

Makes about 40 burekas

INGREDIENTS

CHEESE FILLING

½ cup farmer's, cottage, or ricotta cheese

1 large egg, lightly beaten

1 cup finely grated cheddar cheese

¼ cup (2 ounces) cream cheese

⅛ teaspoon salt

Pinch of ground nutmeg

Pinch of ground white pepper

8 sheets filo dough, cut lengthwise into 3-inch strips

½ cup (1 stick) butter, or vegan spread, melted

SPINACH FILLING

12 ounces fresh spinach, chopped

1 large egg, lightly beaten

1 cup finely grated Swiss or cheddar cheese

2 tablespoons feta or cream cheese

Dash of ground nutmeg

Generous sprinkle of black pepper

When I lived in Jerusalem, Friday and Saturday morning meant homemade burekas, little triangular pastries filled with cheese or spinach, baked by Bulgarian, Turkish, and other Baltic immigrants and eaten by children with hot chocolate and by adults with strong coffee. With filo dough, burekas are easy to make and can be prepared ahead for snacks. They can even be served at adult cocktail parties and passed around by the children, who are proud to claim credit for making them.

Tips: When I make these with children, I use both fillings, making about 20 of each. If you prefer one filling over the other, then double that filling. I often mold them, freeze them on a cookie sheet, and then transfer them to plastic bags. When I want to serve them, I bake them as below.

Adult: Preheat the oven to 350 degrees and line a baking sheet with parchment paper.

Child: To make the cheese filling, mash the farmer's, cottage, or ricotta cheese in a bowl with a fork until it's crumbly. Mix in the egg, cheddar cheese, cream cheese, salt, nutmeg, and white pepper. Blend well.

Child: To make the spinach filling, wash the spinach well, rinsing two or three times. Place it in a saucepan with just the water that clings to the leaves after washing. Cover tightly, and cook the spinach over medium heat until it's tender, about 4 or 5 minutes. Remove the spinach, place it in a strainer, and press out the remaining water with the back of a spoon. Chop the spinach finely into a wooden bowl. Mix well with the egg, cheeses, nutmeg, and pepper.

EQUIPMENT

Mixing bowl
Measuring cup
Measuring spoon
Fork
Pastry brush
Saucepan with lid
Strainer
Wooden bowl
Large spoon
Pancake turner
Baking sheet
Parchment sheet

Child with Adult: Brush a filo strip with butter or vegan spread, and spread 1 heaping teaspoon of the cheese or spinach filling in a corner. Fold over as you would fold a flag to make a triangle, then fold again to make a another triangle, and so forth. Using a pancake turner, place the formed burekas on a baking sheet lined with parchment paper. Brush the top with butter. Repeat with the remaining filling and the remaining filo dough.

Adult: Bake for about 15 minutes, until golden. Eat immediately, or refrigerate and reheat the next morning for Shabbat breakfast.

Serves 4

INGREDIENTS

- 2 scallions
- 2 small red bell peppers
- 2 tablespoons olive oil
- 3 medium tomatoes or a 15.5 ounce can chopped tomatoes
- ½ teaspoon sweet paprika
- ½ teaspoon ground cumin
- ½ teaspoon coriander
- 4 eggs
- 2 ounces cream cheese or feta
- Salt and freshly ground pepper, to taste
- 2 tablespoons chopped cilantro

EQUIPMENT

- Sharp knife
- Medium frying pan with lid
- Measuring spoon
- Grater
- Mixing bowl
- Spoon
- Egg beater

SHAKSHUKA (EGGS IN TOMATO SAUCE)

Shakshuka is one of those onomatopoeic words in Arabic and Hebrew—a word that sounds like what it is. It means, literally, mixed up, which is what you do in this North African recipe for scrambled or poached eggs in a spicy tomato sauce, which came to Israel with Libyan Jews. Making eggs is an American Sunday-morning family ritual that is a pleasure to share with your children. This recipe is a great way for them to learn how to make scrambled or poached eggs. You know your family best, so let the kids add their favorite vegetables and cheeses, from cheddar to feta, and their favorite spices such as paprika, cumin, and ground coriander, the dried seed of fresh coriander (cilantro).

Adult with Child: Cut up the scallions and red peppers into small pieces.

Adult: In a medium frying pan with a lid, quickly sauté the scallions and peppers (and any other vegetables you choose) in the olive oil until the vegetables are soft.

Adult with Child: Cut up the fresh tomatoes into small pieces and put into a bowl.

Adult with Child: Add the tomato liquid and pulp to the vegetables, with the paprika, cumin, and coriander. Cover and cook over low heat for 20 minutes.

Adult with Child: Either beat the eggs well and pour them over the vegetables in the pan or break each egg individually and poach them in the sauce. Add dollops of cream cheese or crumbled feta cheese. Using a fork, gently scramble the eggs well. Then cover the pan and cook for 3 to 4 minutes, until the eggs are set. Season with salt and pepper, sprinkle with the cilantro, and serve with a spoon. Do not overcook.

Note: Among the many possible variations, you can add a minced clove of garlic, an avocado, or whichever cheese you want.

GOLDA MEIR'S CHOCOLATE CHIP COOKIES

Makes about 36

INGREDIENTS

1 cup (2 sticks) unsalted butter, vegan spread, or coconut oil

½ cup granulated sugar

½ cup firmly packed light-brown sugar

1¾ cups unbleached all-purpose flour

1 teaspoon baking soda

1 teaspoon salt

2 large eggs

2 teaspoons orange juice

12 ounces bittersweet chocolate chips

EQUIPMENT

Measuring cups

Measuring spoons

Mixing bowls

Wooden spoon

Stand mixer

2 baking sheets

Parchment paper

Pancake turner

Cooling rack

Golda Meir was born in Kiev, Ukraine, and came to Milwaukee, Wisconsin, at eighteen. She later decided to live on a kibbutz in Israel, where she eventually became the prime minister and a heroine to women around the world. Even while she led her country, she entertained friends and visitors in her simple kitchen. One of her favorite foods, linking America and Israel, was chocolate chip cookies, which she varied by adding Jaffa orange juice to the classic recipe she had learned in Wisconsin.

Adult: Preheat the oven to 350 degrees, and cover two baking sheets with parchment paper.

Child with Adult: Using a wooden spoon or a stand mixer, cream together the butter, vegan spread, or coconut oil and the two sugars.

Child: In another bowl, mix the flour, baking soda, and salt. Add the flour mixture to the butter and sugar, stir in the eggs and orange juice, and beat or mix until everything is smooth and well combined. (If you beat by hand, take turns at it—it's fun.) Stir in the chocolate chips.

Child: Drop the dough by tablespoonsful onto the baking sheets, and flatten them slightly with your palm. Keep them about 3 inches apart.

Adult: Bake for 10 to 12 minutes, or until the cookies are golden. Remove them from the oven, and let them sit a few minutes to cool slightly.

Child: When they're ready, transfer with a pancake turner to a rack to cool.

Makes 2 loaves or 24 cookies

INGREDIENTS

1 cup (2 sticks) unsalted butter, vegan spread, or coconut oil, at room temperature

1 cup plus 2 teaspoons sugar

4 large eggs

1 teaspoon vanilla extract

½ cup orange juice

4 cups unbleached all-purpose flour

2 teaspoons baking powder

1 teaspoon salt

2 cups bittersweet chocolate chips

1 cup grated coconut

½ cup chopped almonds or pecans (optional)

¼ teaspoon ground cinnamon

EQUIPMENT

Measuring cups

Measuring spoons

Mixing bowls

Stand mixer

Whisk or large spoon

Two 5-by-10-inch loaf pans

Serrated knife

Baking sheets

Parchment paper

MANDELBROT

When my husband was growing up, his mother always made special cookies for the Sabbath. She would bake them, then slice them and bake them again, sprinkled with cinnamon sugar. Do they sound a lot like biscotti, which means "twice baked"? They are. We've added chocolate chips to our modern version.

Adult: Preheat the oven to 350 degrees, and line the loaf pans with parchment paper that extends over the edges of the pans.

Child with Adult: Put the butter, vegan spread, or coconut oil, and 1 cup of the sugar in the bowl of a stand mixer with the paddle attachment. In a separate small bowl, using a whisk or large spoon, beat the eggs well. Then add the eggs to the mixer with the vanilla and orange juice. »

Mandelbrot continued »

Child: In another bowl, mix together the flour, baking powder, and salt. Add this to the other ingredients, and turn on the machine.

Child: Carefully blend in the chocolate chips, coconut, and, if using, nuts. Spoon half the dough into each pan, and bake them for about 50 minutes, or until a toothpick comes out clean and the top is hard to the touch. Cool them for a few minutes in the pan, cut them into ½-inch slices, and carefully lift them in the parchment paper from the pans.

Adult: Turn up the oven to 400 degrees.

Child with Adult: Arrange the mandelbrot slices down flat on the baking sheets. Mix the cinnamon with the remaining 2 teaspoons sugar, and sprinkle this over the top. Brown the slices in the oven for about 15 minutes, or until they're golden and crisp.

Havdalah

Havdalah, the ceremony marking the close of the Sabbath at sunset, is one of the nicest aspects of Shabbat for children. It reflects the real "spice and spirit" of the Sabbath. As soon as the first stars are seen in the sky, the Havdalah candle is lit. Unlike the two separate candles ushering in the Sabbath, the Havdalah candle has at least two and usually three entwined wicks, which come together to strengthen it, just as we enter the new week with the experience of Shabbat strengthening us. You can make your own Havdalah candles. Just use three long, very thin candles. Dip them in hot water, braid them together, and hold them together with foil at the bottom. (Younger children can also do this with licorice sticks.) This is a project in which older children can help younger ones.

After the candle is lit, there is a blessing over the wine, which symbolizes joy. Then the spices are blessed. Make this seasonal in your home. Pick flowers or aromatic herbs from your garden in the summer, and let your children select spices from a health food store's bulk bins in winter. The spices, most often cinnamon and cloves, symbolize the spiritual riches of the Sabbath and are sniffed before they're replaced in the receptacle—in a child's case, a matchbox, film container, or pill bottle. A child can also pierce an orange or an apple with cloves, as my father did on Yom Kippur in Germany, to sniff to keep the hunger away. These spices are also to cheer the soul—so saddened by the departure of the Sabbath.

ROSH HASHANAH

Australian Carrot Dip 50

Moroccan Apricot Chicken Tagine 51

Sort of Sephardic Sweet Potatoes, Chickpeas, and Squash 54

Peeling a Pomegranate 57

Persian Pomegranate Punch 58

Crustless Quiche with Cherry Tomatoes, Basil, and Cheese 59

Apple Cake Eden 60

Rosh Hashanah Dinner

Round Challah*

Australian Carrot Dip*

Apple Slices Dipped in Honey

Chicken Soup with Matzo Balls*

Moroccan Apricot Chicken Tagine*

Rice or Couscous

Sort of Sephardic Sweet Potatoes, Chickpeas, and Squash*

Apple Cake Eden*

Rosh Hashanah Lunch

Round Challah*

Golden Harvest Tzimmes*

Brisket

Chopped Israeli Salad*

Apple-Honey Cupcakes*

ROSH HASHANAH

Rosh Hashanah, literally "head of the year," is the Jewish New Year celebrating the birthday of the world. To our family, it means not only the beginning of school, but the beginning of a new yearly cycle and the Jewish belief in the possibility of renewal and goodness. We like to think of the symbolism of the food at this time of year. No dark foods—only bright and fresh oranges, carrots, honey, apples. Circles symbolize a good year all year round, as our earth is round. We shape our challah into a circle for Rosh Hashanah, sometimes adding golden raisins in hope of an even sweeter year. We always start our meal with apples dipped in honey, pomegranates (now so plentiful at this time of year), and those wonderful California dates, all symbolic of the new fruit in the land of the Bible and in our world. We say the following prayer over all of these fruits:

Baruch atah Adonai Eloheinu melech ha-olam, shehecheyanu, ve-kiyemanu, ve-higianu, laz-man ha-zeh.

Blessed art Thou, Adonai, our God, who has kept us alive, sustained us, and enabled us to reach this special day.

Our dinner on the eve of the holiday is a rather hurried affair, between coming home from school and work and rushing off to synagogue. The luncheon after Rosh Hashanah morning services is our time for a real feast, to which we invite friends and family; we often make it a potluck.

Serves 4 to 6

INGREDIENTS

1 pound carrots

½ small red onion

2 cloves garlic, peeled

2 tablespoons olive oil

1 teaspoon ground coriander

3 tablespoons chopped fresh cilantro or parsley

1 tablespoon lemon juice

1 tablespoon honey, or to taste

Salt and pepper, to taste

Harissa, to taste

EQUIPMENT

Vegetable peeler

Knife

Microplane

Medium bowl

Frying pan large enough to hold the carrots

Wooden spoon

Measuring spoons

Blender

Serving bowl

Storage bowl with a cover

AUSTRALIAN CARROT DIP

When I visited Melbourne and Sydney recently, every Shabbat dinner included three dips with the challahs: chopped liver, chopped egg, and hummus or this carrot dip. It's delicious to eat any time during the year, but especially at Rosh Hashanah, when we welcome the New Year and enjoy the carrots' robustness. Sliced carrots look like gold coins because of their color, making this a triply symbolic dish for the New Year—round, brightly colored, and sweet. What better way for my children and now my grandchildren to eat vegetables! When I asked the owners of Lox Stock & Barrel in Bondi Beach, they said their catering chef, Damien, was "very chuffed" (very pleased) to pass the recipe on to me.

Child with Adult: Peel the carrots, remove the stems, and cut each into three pieces, making sure to hold the carrots carefully with one hand while cutting with the other. Cut the red onion into chunks, and shave the garlic with a microplane. Put everything into a medium bowl.

Adult: Heat the olive oil in the frying pan, add the carrot mixture, and cook for about 15 minutes, until the carrots are tender. While the carrots are cooking, add the ground coriander, 2 tablespoons of the cilantro or parsley, the lemon juice, honey, and salt and pepper to taste, and stir in the harissa, making sure the amount of heat is to your children's taste. Have them discuss the final flavor with you.

Child Alone or with Adult: When the carrots are cool enough to handle, purée them in a blender. Scrape into a storage bowl. Cover the bowl with its cover and refrigerate for at least 6 hours, stirring occasionally to blend the flavors.

Adult: Serve the dip in a pretty bowl, sprinkled with the last tablespoon of cilantro or parsley, as the first course on a Friday night with challah.

MOROCCAN APRICOT CHICKEN TAGINE

Serves 6 to 8

INGREDIENTS

¼ cup vegetable oil

2 medium onions, sliced into thin rings

One 3½- to 4-pound chicken, cut into 8 pieces

Salt and freshly ground black pepper, to taste

1 teaspoon ground cinnamon

1 teaspoon ground coriander

1 teaspoon ground ginger

1 cup dried apricots

¼ cup raisins

Big pinch of saffron

½ teaspoon ground cumin

½ teaspoon hot paprika

½ cup almonds

Cooked rice or couscous, for serving

Chopped parsley or cilantro for garnish (optional)

EQUIPMENT

Measuring cups

Measuring spoons

Tagine or Dutch oven

Mixing bowl

Colander

Small pan

Nonstick skillet

Cooking is always a geography lesson—especially for children like mine, who remember our family vacation to Morocco, where we had this tagine at Friday-night dinner with a Jewish family in Marrakech. A tagine is a kind of Dutch oven in a triangular form. The dish cooked within it is sprinkled with ras el hanout, meaning "top of the spices," in this country that is literally the end of the ancient spice route. Can you imagine twelve spices in a mixture? Have your children make their own mixture of their favorite spices to sprinkle on this delicious dish. »

Moroccan Apricot Chicken Tagine continued »

Adult: Heat the oil in a Dutch oven or other large, heavy frying pan with a cover. Add the onions, and sauté slowly over medium heat until they're golden.

Child: While the onions are cooking, season the chicken pieces well with salt and pepper, and sprinkle with the cinnamon, coriander, and ginger.

Adult with Child: Push the onions to the sides of the pan, and tuck in the chicken pieces. Brown them well on all sides.

Child with Adult: Sprinkle the apricots and raisins over the chicken pieces, along with the saffron, cumin, paprika, and 1 cup of water. Simmer, covered, stirring occasionally, for about 40 minutes, or until the chicken is cooked and most of the liquid has evaporated. (Add more water if necessary.)

Adult with Child: While the chicken is cooking, bring a small pan of water to a boil, and add the almonds; keep them in the boiling water for only a minute or two to blanch them. Drain them in a colander, and when they are cool enough to hold, have the child pinch the peels off the almonds. Sometimes the almonds will just pop out across the table; it's lots of fun. Then dry the blanched almonds and toast them until they're slightly golden in a nonstick skillet. Just before serving, sprinkle them over the chicken. Add chopped parsley or cilantro for garnish, if you choose. Serve with rice or couscous.

SORT OF SEPHARDIC SWEET POTATOES, CHICKPEAS, AND SQUASH

Serves 6

INGREDIENTS

5 tablespoons extra-virgin olive oil

2 large onions

1 pound butternut squash

1 pound sweet potatoes or yams

One 15-ounce can chickpeas, drained

¼ cup dried cranberries or cherries

2 tablespoons brown sugar

½ teaspoon salt

½ teaspoon ground ginger

1 teaspoon ground cinnamon

2 tablespoons chopped parsley or cilantro

EQUIPMENT

Vegetable peeler

Sharp paring knife

Food processor

Wooden spoon

Frying pan

Mixing bowl

Aluminum foil

Oblong casserole dish (about 9 by 13 inches)

Measuring spoons

Measuring cup

Sephardic Jews from Turkey, Greece, Morocco, and other countries of the Mediterranean region say seven special blessings over seven different symbolic foods at their Rosh Hashanah dinner. Five of these blessings are over fruits and vegetables—apples (candied or dipped in sugar or honey), leeks, beet greens or spinach, dates, and zucchini or squash. (The other two species are barley and wheat.) These blessings symbolize their hopes for the New Year. Many of these Jews trace their ancestors back to Spain, which is called Sepharad. Over the centuries, the Sephardic Jews took advantage of the abundance of vegetables available in the Mediterranean countries, often throughout the year. Among these vegetables are sweet potatoes and squash, great favorites in my family. The special blessing you can say over your sweet potatoes and squash at the beginning of your Rosh Hashanah dinner goes like this:

Yehi ratzon mi-le-faneha Adonai Eloheinu ve-lo-hei avoteinu she-tik-rah ro-a gezar dinenu ve-yi-karehu lefa-neha za-hee-yo-teinu.

May it be thy will, Adonai, our God and God of our fathers, that you should tear up any evil decree and let only our merits be read before You.

Adult: Preheat the oven to 375 degrees and grease a 9-by-13-inch casserole dish with a tablespoon of the olive oil.

Adult with Child: Chop the onions, either by hand or in a food processor. Heat a large frying pan with a cover, add 2 more tablespoons olive oil, and sauté the onions until they're golden.

Adult: While the onions are cooking, peel the squash.

Child: While the adults are peeling the squash, the children should use a vegetable peeler to peel the sweet potatoes or yams.

Child with Adult: Then carefully cut both the sweet potatoes and squash into 1-inch cubes and set them aside.

Child: Scatter the chickpeas on top of the onions on the bottom of the casserole. Cover with the squash and sweet potatoes, then the dried cranberries or cherries, and finish with the brown sugar, salt, ginger, cinnamon, and ½ cup of water. Drizzle with the remaining 2 tablespoons olive oil if you like.

Adult: Bake, covered, for 20 minutes, and another 20 minutes uncovered. Have the children peek to see when the dish is well browned. Serve it sprinkled with parsley or cilantro.

Pomegranates

One of the fruits mentioned most often in the Biblical and Jewish liturgy is the pomegranate, which legend says has 613 arils in each, the same as the number of Jewish commandments, or Mitzvot, in the Bible. They may sometimes have 613 but my daughter Merissa counted 498 in one. Many people even think that the Tree of Life was a pomegranate tree—the French name, *grenade,* means "apple with seeds."

In our family, we like pomegranates in a variety of ways. We eat the seeds individually as a snack, we sprinkle them on cereal, we put them over grapefruit and orange sections in fruit cups, and we drink the juice alone or mixed with grapefruit and orange juice.

As far as I am concerned, Persians know more about pomegranates than anyone else, since pomegranates come from Iran. Jews from Iran have taught me how to peel a pomegranate, and how their children drink the juice straight from the fruit or—to be more accurate—suck the juice out from the fruit. We added a straw and called it Pomegranate Punch. It's been a big hit with my children and now my grandchildren. Try it.

INGREDIENTS

1 smooth red pomegranate

EQUIPMENT

1 sharp paring knife

1 small or 1 huge mixing bowl

Sieve or strainer

PEELING A POMEGRANATE

Adult: Using a sharp knife, score the top of the pomegranate where there are natural humps, making 1-inch-long incisions.

Child: Carefully peel off the pomegranate skin, and even more carefully remove the arils with your fingers to a small bowl. Or, to ensure that no squirts of pomegranate juice spot your house, fill a huge mixing bowl with cold water. Once you have scored the pomegranate, place it in the bowl. Roll up your sleeves and grasp the pomegranate under the water. Remove the skin, then the arils, or pods, covering the seeds which will fall to the bottom of the bowl. Once you have finished, drain off the water, and you will have plump, delicious pomegranate seeds. Eat them as they are, or make juice from them.

Adult with Child: To make juice, place the pomegranate seeds in a sieve over a small mixing bowl. Using your hands, press as hard as you can to extract the juice. Be careful to wash your hands right away afterward.

Note: You can also just cut the pomegranate in half and tap gently but firmly with a hammer; the seeds will fall out into a bowl.

Serves 1

INGREDIENTS

1 pomegranate

EQUIPMENT

1 shish kebab skewer
1 straw

PERSIAN POMEGRANATE PUNCH

Child: Take a smooth pomegranate and roll it on a countertop, bearing down as much as you can without breaking the skin, until all the crunchy sounds stop. You will have to do this over the whole surface of the pomegranate. It will take a while, but it is great fun. Once it is soft all around and there is no crunchiness left, give the pomegranate to an adult.

Adult: Place the pomegranate on the table, take a shish kebab skewer, and gently make a hole in the pomegranate. Quickly take a straw and insert it into the hole. You may have to suck out some of the juice since it may spurt out.

Child: Drink the pomegranate juice through the straw. It is delicious. It may take a few seconds for the juice to come into the straw, but it is worth waiting for!

Note: This is also another good way to extract pomegranate juice for recipes.

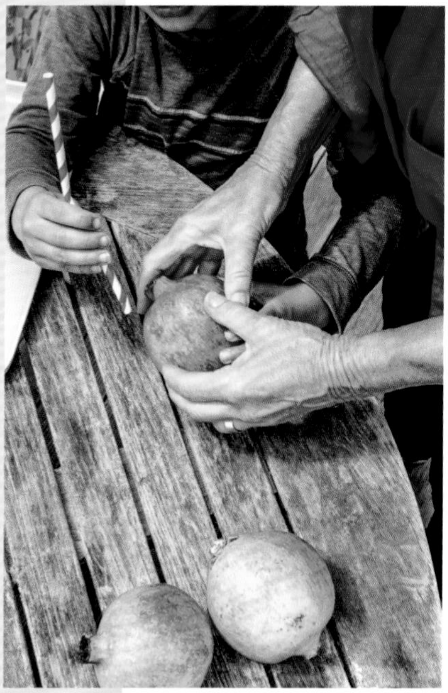

CRUSTLESS QUICHE WITH CHERRY TOMATOES, BASIL, AND CHEESE

Makes 1 quiche, serving 6 to 8

INGREDIENTS

¼ cup whole fresh basil leaves

1 tablespoon olive oil

6 large eggs

3 heaping tablespoons crème fraîche

1 cup milk

⅓ cup crumbled goat cheese

4 tablespoons grated Parmesan cheese

3 tablespoons all-purpose flour

1 teaspoon salt

Freshly ground black pepper, to taste

2 pints cherry or grape tomatoes

EQUIPMENT

One 9-inch quiche mold or springform pan

Parchment paper

Small cup

Measuring spoons

Measuring cups

Whisk

Medium bowl

Toothpick

I love this dish; cherry tomatoes—still so sweet at the time of Rosh Hashanah, in the fall—and basil add such brightness, and it's easy to cook. I discovered it at a farmers' market in Paris a few years ago. Now I also slip sautéed mushrooms or spinach into this yummy dish for my grandchildren. Without a crust, it is easy to make, looks beautiful, and is child-friendly, during the week and for holidays or the Sabbath. It is also a dish that even very young children, with supervision, can make themselves.

Child with Adult: Line the bottom and sides of a 9-inch quiche mold or springform pan with parchment paper.

Then put the basil leaves in a small cup with the olive oil, and let them sit while you're preparing the quiche.

Break the eggs into a medium bowl. Then stir in the crème fraîche, milk, goat cheese, Parmesan cheese, flour, salt, and freshly ground pepper to taste, making sure you whisk enough so there are no more lumps of flour.

Put the cherry tomatoes in the prepared pan, pour the egg mixture over them, and poke the basil leaves into the mixture.

Place the quiche in a cold oven, and then heat it to 350 degrees. Cook for about 45 minutes, or until a toothpick comes out clean and the quiche starts to turn slightly golden on top. Serve immediately or at room temperature.

APPLE CAKE EDEN

Makes 1 cake, serving 6 to 8

INGREDIENTS

1¼ cups unbleached all-purpose flour

¼ teaspoon salt

1 teaspoon baking powder

½ cup unsalted butter, vegan spread, or coconut oil

Grated zest of 1 large lemon

1 large egg yolk

1 cup sugar

2 pounds (about 5) Granny Smith or other tart yet flavorful apples

1 teaspoon ground cinnamon

EQUIPMENT

9-inch springform pan

Measuring cups

Measuring spoons

Mixing bowl

Spoon

Dough cutter

Grater or food processor

Apple corer

Vegetable peeler

Sieve

Spatula

Parchment paper

Dull knife

Baking sheet

This is a very simple and simply delicious cake, one of my favorites. I dubbed it Apple Cake Eden, but you can call it whatever you like. Just make sure that the children design an apple on top of the cake—or whatever they want! (They may have to change the name, however.)

Adult with Child: Preheat the oven to 425 degrees, and line a 9-inch springform pan with parchment paper.

Child with Adult: Using either a food processor, or a bowl and your hands, mix the flour, salt, baking powder, and butter, vegan spread, or coconut oil until crumbly. Then zest the lemon, and add the zest with the egg yolk and ¼ cup of the sugar. Mold it into a ball, and set it aside.

Adult with Child: Using a vegetable peeler and an apple corer, peel and core the apples. Then, using a grater or the food processor or a mixture of both, grate the apples, and mix them with the remaining ¾ cup of sugar and the cinnamon. Transfer this mixture to a sieve over a mixing bowl, and let it sit for 20 minutes.

Child with Adult: Cut the dough with a dough cutter into two pieces, three-quarters and one-quarter of the dough. Take the larger part and press into the top and sides of the springform pan.

Child: With a large spoon, move the drained apples to the dough in the pan, using a spatula to flatten the apples. Then roll or press out the leftover quarter of the dough, and cut it with a dull knife to make a decorative apple or whatever design you want; place it in the center of the apple-strewn dough.

Adult: Bake in the middle of the oven, on top of a cookie sheet (for spills), for 15 minutes, then reduce the oven to 350 degrees for another 30 minutes, or until the crust is golden.

YOM KIPPUR

Lekoach 68
Yemenite High Holy Day Soup 69
Kreplach 71
Mushroom Kreplach Dumplings 72
Apple-Honey Cupcakes 73
Greek Lemonade 74
Lentil, Squash, and Carrot Soup 76

Yemenite Dinner Before the Fast

Lekoach*

Yemenite High Holy Day Soup*

Apple-Honey Cupcakes*

Eastern European Dinner Before the Fast

Chicken Soup with Kreplach*

Roast Chicken

Rice

Mandelbrot*

Break-the-Fast Menu

Persian Pomegranate Punch*

Greek Lemonade*

Apple Slices Dipped in Honey

Round Challah*

Bagels*

Lentil, Squash, and Carrot Soup*

Apple and Cream Cheese Spread*

Aunt Lorraine's Noodle Kugel*

Tzatziki*

Bread Furst Brownies*

YOM KIPPUR

Yom Kippur, the Day of Atonement, is a day of fasting and repentance from dusk to dusk for twenty-four hours. This holiest day of the Jewish year is not a time to think about cooking—but our family does, especially to break the fast. When they were young, the children helped me make a break-the-fast for family and friends.

In this country, a dairy meal, often a glorified brunch with bagels, lox, cream cheese, herring, kugel, and such, is served to break the fast, beginning with coffee, or tea, and a sweet—sometimes an apple dipped in honey or a piece of honey cake—followed by herring or another salty food. From there on, it is up to the imagination or the background of the hosts. Russian or German Jews often make schnecken (sticky buns; I included a recipe in *Jewish Cooking in America*); Moroccans, fijuelas (deep-fried pastries oozing with honey); Syrians, Iranians, and Egyptians, a cardamom cake; and Yemenites, a ginger cake. Quinces, pomegranates, watermelon, dates, or other seasonal fruits are also served.

LEKOACH

Serves 8 to 10

INGREDIENTS

- 1 tablespoon active dry yeast
- 1 tablespoon sugar
- 3 cups unbleached all-purpose flour
- 1 tablespoon salt
- ½ cup vegetable oil

EQUIPMENT

- Measuring spoons
- Measuring cups
- Large mixing bowl
- Spoon
- Clean dish towel
- Dutch oven

Many years ago, when I lived in Jerusalem, I started the fast of Yom Kippur with Yemenite Jews. We all sat on the floor on little pillows and began our meal with a Sabbath flatbread called lekoach, which I had once seen cooked on a flat frying pan at a Yemenite moshav in Israel. Later, during the meal, we dipped the bread into a yummy soup with meat, chicken, and many spices. The symbolic food, in large bowls all around the table, included robust pomegranates. Some say Yemenite Jews separated from the ancient Israelites when they were all wandering for forty years in the desert, veering off and heading south to the Arabian Peninsula, near Ethiopia. Others say the Queen of Sheba brought the Abyssinians, which included today's Yemenites and Ethiopians, back with her from Jerusalem. Even though Yemenite Jews were separated from the Jews of Europe and the Middle East for more than two thousand years, they still observe many of the same customs, including using a bread to start each holiday meal. This holiday bread, lekoach, is made in a frying pan. Here I call for a Dutch oven, but a large cast-iron skillet with a lid would work equally well.

Adult with Child: In a bowl, mix together the yeast, 1 cup of water, and the sugar, and make sure it bubbles. Then gradually add the flour and salt, and knead until everything is well mixed. Cover the dough with a clean towel, and let it rise for about 2 hours.

Adult: Pour the oil into the Dutch oven over low heat on the stovetop. Roll the dough into a circle large enough to fit in the Dutch oven, and put it into the pot. Cook it, covered, for 1 hour or until the bottom of the bread is golden brown. Turn the bread and cook for another half hour, until fully browned on both sides. Serve hot, dipped in soup or hot sauce.

YEMENITE HIGH HOLY DAY SOUP

Serves 10 to 12

INGREDIENTS

- 3 celery stalks
- 1 medium zucchini
- 3 carrots
- 1 large tomato
- 2 medium russet potatoes, peeled
- One 3-pound chicken, cleaned and quartered
- 1 quart beef broth
- 10 to 12 cloves garlic, peeled
- 2 onions
- 2 leeks
- 1 large white turnip, quartered but unpeeled
- 1 small bunch fresh parsley or cilantro, chopped
- Salt, to taste
- 1 tablespoon hawayij, or to taste (see note on page 70 for how to make the spice blend)

EQUIPMENT

- Storage cups, for refrigerating
- Large soup pot or casserole with a cover
- Slotted spoon

My mother-in-law would often describe the *kapparah* tradition in Poland. Early in the morning of the day prior to Yom Kippur, she whirled a live chicken over her head, while she thought about turning over a new leaf. Her father would whirl a rooster, her mother a hen, and her brothers and sisters a pullet (a young hen) or a cockerel (a young rooster). The ceremony was repeated separately for each child. She was always frightened by the fluttering feathers. After the whirling, her mother would race to the *shohet* and have the fowls ritually slaughtered to make food for the meal before the fast. All the fowl would be cooked, and any extras given to bachelor relatives or to the poor. Chicken soup would be made for the kreplach, and the boiled chicken would be eaten as a mild-flavored main dish.

Yemenite Jews also eat chicken before the fast of Yom Kippur, but much earlier in the day, at about ten-thirty. They dip lekoach into their soup, which is flavored with spices and lots of vegetables. I've simplified this recipe by using beef broth rather than the beef stew and marrow bones used in a traditional Yemenite kitchen.

Child with Adult: Cut the celery, zucchini, carrots, tomato, and potatoes into about 1-inch pieces. Store all of them, except the potatoes, in a covered container in the refrigerator until you need them. Store the potatoes, covered in cold water, in a separate container, or they will turn a terrible gray color.

Adult with Child: Place the chicken in a large pot with the beef broth and enough water to almost cover it. Bring the liquid to a boil, lower the heat, and simmer until a froth forms. Skim the froth off with a slotted spoon, which is a very satisfying thing to do.

Adult with Child: Lower the heat, and add the garlic cloves. Peel and cut the onions into chunks. Cut the leeks in half lengthwise, then run them under water to remove any grit. Then cut into chunks. Add the onions, turnip, and leeks. Cook, covered, about 1 hour, or until the meat seems fairly tender.

Adult: Let the soup cool, and refrigerate for a few hours or overnight. »

Yemenite High Holy Day Soup continued »

Child with Adult: If you want, skim the fat off the soup, but Yemenite Jews do not necessarily do so. Remove the chicken and discard the skin and the bones, then tear the meat into pieces and return it to the broth. Bring the soup back to a boil. Add the celery, zucchini, carrots, tomato, and potatoes. Lower the heat, cover, and simmer for another 20 minutes. Just before serving, add the parsley or cilantro, salt, and hawayij, adding more or less to taste, and cook, covered, for a few more minutes.

Adult: Adjust the seasonings.

Eat by dipping the lekoach bread (page 68) into the soup and scooping up the meat, vegetables, and the liquid. Serve with rice if you like.

Note: Making a children's version of hawayij is a great way to introduce them to Middle Eastern spices. Take the children to a spice store where they can pick out the spices themselves. Hawayij is a combination of cumin, coriander (omit if you're using fresh cilantro instead of parsley), curry powder, ginger, black pepper, and turmeric. Add spices according to your children's tolerance for strong flavors. You can omit them altogether if you wish.

Makes about 60

INGREDIENTS

FILLING

- 1 small onion, chopped
- ¾ pound ground beef, chicken, turkey, or mushrooms
- 1 large egg
- Salt and pepper, to taste

NOODLE DOUGH

- 3 large eggs
- ¾ teaspoon salt
- 2 cups unbleached all-purpose flour, or more as needed

EQUIPMENT

- Frying pan
- Wooden spoon
- Mixing bowl
- Fork
- Clean, moist towel
- Rolling pin
- Knife
- Measuring spoons
- Measuring cup
- Large pot of boiling water
- Slotted spoon

KREPLACH

Kreplach—often called Jewish wontons—are traditional for the meal before the fast at Yom Kippur. Kreplach are also eaten on Simchat Torah and Purim. Here is our recipe. Children love making noodles! They often turn out in varied shapes—no matter; they taste good and we feel great making them ourselves. The meat filling can be beef, chicken, or turkey.

TO MAKE THE FILLING

Adult: Set a frying pan over medium heat and sauté the onion with the ground meat or mushrooms until the meat is cooked through. Pour off excess fat. Let the mixture cool slightly.

Child: Mix the egg into the meat or mushrooms. Add as much salt and pepper as you like.

TO MAKE THE NOODLES

Child with Adult: Using a fork, lightly beat the eggs in a mixing bowl. Add the salt, 2 tablespoons of water, and enough flour to make a medium-soft dough. Knead well and quickly by hand. Divide the dough into two balls. Cover them with a moist towel.

Adult, then Child: Working quickly, roll out one ball of dough very thin with a rolling pin and cut it into six strips, each 1½ inches wide. Then cut the strips into 1½-inch squares.

Child: Place ½ teaspoon meat mixture on each square. Fold each into a triangle and press the edges together firmly, using water on your fingers to make them stick. Press together two of the ends. Repeat with the second ball of dough.

Child: Drop the kreplach into boiling water, and cook, uncovered, for 15 minutes. Remove them with a slotted spoon and put them into chicken soup.

MUSHROOM KREPLACH DUMPLINGS

Makes about 50 dumplings

INGREDIENTS

FILLING FOR THE WRAPPERS

- 4 cups fresh mushrooms (shiitake, cremini, or portobello) (about 1 pound)
- 2 large sweet shallots
- 1 tablespoon roasted sesame oil
- Splash of Shaoxing wine
- 1 package Japanese gyoza wrappers or wonton wrappers

DIPPING SAUCE

- ½ cup soy sauce
- ¼ cup white vinegar
- 2 tablespoons brown sugar
- 2 tablespoons roasted sesame oil

EQUIPMENT

- Measuring cups
- Measuring spoons
- Sharp knife or food processor
- Small bowl
- Large bowl
- Medium frying pan
- Chinese spoon strainer
- Large pot

Tara Lazar makes a yummy shortcut vegan version of mushroom kreplach dumplings. Tara, a mother, restaurant owner, and marvelous cook, whose mother was Chinese and whose father was Jewish, often invites adults and children to her house to help finish these dumplings—a perfect icebreaker for all. Although her dad liked traditional kreplach, these mushroom dumplings always remind her of her mom, who often made them instead of kreplach.

Adult with Child: Chop the mushrooms and then the shallots very finely. You want them too fine for young children to chop, but children can use the food processor, pulsing on and off until the mushrooms and then the shallots are finely chopped. Separate them into two bowls.

Adult with Child: Heat the sesame oil for the filling in a medium frying pan, and sauté the shallots in it until they are translucent. Add the Shaoxing wine, then add the chopped mushrooms, and continue cooking until the liquid has cooked off. Remove the mushroom filling from the pan, and place it in a strainer over a bowl.

Adult Showing Child: Put a tablespoon of filling into a wrapper and, with your fingertip, run water around the edge of the wrapper to seal. Fold the dough in two to make a semicircle. Holding the dumpling in one hand, run your finger across the half-moon to seal it tightly, and push the air out with the other.

Adult with Child: In a large pot, bring the water to a boil and drop the dumplings in, about twelve at a time. Cook them for about 2 minutes, or until they float to the top—let the children watch them come up to the top.

Child: While the dumplings are cooking, make the dipping sauce by stirring the soy sauce, white vinegar, brown sugar, and sesame oil together and giving it a good stir until the brown sugar is dissolved.

Child: Once the dumplings are starting to float, remove them with an Asian spoon strainer so you can have the boiling water ready for the next round. Let the dumplings cool a little, dip them into the sauce, and eat. Yum!

APPLE-HONEY CUPCAKES

Makes 18

INGREDIENTS

- ¼ cup vegetable oil
- ¾ cup honey
- 2 large eggs, well beaten
- 2 cups unbleached all-purpose flour
- 1 teaspoon baking powder
- 1 teaspoon baking soda
- 1 teaspoon salt
- 2 cups coarsely grated raw apples
- 1 teaspoon ground cinnamon
- ½ teaspoon ground nutmeg
- ½ teaspoon ground allspice
- ¼ teaspoon cardamom
- ⅔ cup chopped walnuts (optional)

EQUIPMENT

- Measuring cups
- Measuring spoons
- Mixing bowls
- Wooden spoon
- Sifter
- Paper muffin cups
- Muffin tins

For Eastern European Jews, honey, a reminder of hope for a sweet future, is essential to bring in the New Year.

Adult: Preheat the oven to 350 degrees.

Child: Whisk the oil with the honey in a large bowl. Mix in the eggs. Sift together the flour, baking powder, baking soda, and salt in a separate bowl. Mix the grated apples with the spices and, if using, the walnuts in a small bowl.

Adult with Child: Add a little of the flour mixture to the egg mixture, stirring with a wooden spoon, then a little grated apple, then some more flour mixture, and so on, until all the flour and apple mixtures are incorporated.

Adult with Child: Place the paper muffin cups in the muffin pans, then fill the cups two-thirds full. Bake for about 20 minutes, until light golden brown or until a toothpick inserted in the middle comes out clean. Let cool, and serve plain or smeared with honey.

GREEK LEMONADE

Makes 2 cups

INGREDIENTS

6 lemons, at room temperature

1 cup sugar

1 cup water

Fresh mint, to taste

EQUIPMENT

Knife

Fork

Citrus juicer (optional)

Measuring cup

Saucepan

Spoon

After the final blowing of the shofar, Jews return home to break the fast with food and drink. Customs differ from household to household around the world. What is essential is that the drink be thirst-quenching. In the United States, adults often drink orange juice, coffee, or hot tea. In Greece, depending on what area they come from, Jews sip drinks made from yogurt, almonds, pomegranates, black cherries, pumpkin seeds, or lemons.

Adult: Cut the lemons in half.

Child: Using a fork, pierce the inside of each lemon. If you are right-handed, place the lemon in that hand. Place your left hand palm up over a measuring cup. Squeeze the lemon with your right hand, letting the juice pour through the fingers of your left hand to catch all the seeds, or squeeze the lemons with a juicer.

Adult with Child: Put the sugar and water into a saucepan, and bring it to a boil over medium heat, just until the sugar has dissolved. This will happen very quickly. The child can watch. Cool the syrup. First dilute the lemon juice with some water, then add as much of the sugar syrup as you want to reach the desirable sweetness. Serve cold in tall glasses that have been frosted in the freezer. Add long sprigs of mint for color.

Serves 6 to 8

INGREDIENTS

½ teaspoon curry powder

¼ teaspoon turmeric

¼ teaspoon cumin seeds or ground cumin

½ teaspoon ground coriander

1 small butternut squash or Hokkaido pumpkin

½ cup orange juice

½ cup red lentils (brown will do, too)

1 medium onion

1 celery stalk

2 tablespoons olive oil

Salt, to taste

2 large carrots

½ cup unsweetened coconut milk

Freshly ground black pepper, to taste

Juice of ½ lime

Handful of chopped fresh cilantro or parsley

EQUIPMENT

Measuring spoons

Sharp knife

Mortar and pestle, or blender

Measuring cups

Roasting pan

Bowl

Soup pot or casserole

Carrot peeler

Melon baller or wooden spoon

Perforated spoon

Reamer

Bowls, for serving

Ladle

LENTIL, SQUASH, AND CARROT SOUP

Moroccans serve a delicious *harira,* a bean-and-lentil soup, to break the fast of Yom Kippur. (You can find my children's favorite in *King Solomon's Table,* and another version in *The Foods of Israel Today.*) But my grandchildren prefer this curried lentil soup, which they discovered when they went to the Blossom English-Speaking Preschool of the Arts in Warsaw, Poland. While there, they had four snacks a day, mostly soups that they loved. Alma, especially, liked this creamy soup with red lentils, which Chef Wojtek Gurtiakow thought the children could swallow more easily than other bean soups or ones including the French black lentils. This is a delicious way to break the fast of Yom Kippur, or to eat any day of the year.

Adult with Child: If you want, go to a spice store, pick out fresh spices, grind them together with a mortar and pestle or a blender, and set the mixture aside. Otherwise, have the children measure out the spices, put them into a small bowl, and set that aside.

Adult: Preheat the oven to 400 degrees, and cut the squash or pumpkin down the center in a vertical cut to reveal the seeds. Scrape out the seeds. You can save them to roast for a snack later.

Child: Pour the orange juice into a roasting pan large enough to hold the squash or pumpkin. Set the squash or pumpkin, cut side down, into the pan, and bake for about 30 minutes, until soft.

Adult with Child: Measure out the lentils, and cover them with water. This makes them more easily digestible, according to Chef Wojtek.

Adult with Child: Show the child how to cut the onion and celery carefully into large chunks. They can do it—just be watchful. Then pour the oil into a medium soup pot, and sauté the onion and celery for a few minutes, so that the flavors start to meld. Add half the spice mixture and a bit of salt.

Child: Peel the carrots, and cut them into 1-inch pieces. Throw these into the pot with the onion and celery. Add 5 cups of water, drain the lentils, throw them into the soup pot, and bring the water to a boil. Cook for 15 to 20 minutes, or until the lentils are soft.

Adult with Child: Scoop out the cooked squash pulp with a melon baller or large spoon, and add it to the soup along with the coconut milk. Using a large perforated spoon, remove the vegetables and some liquid to a blender and mix, but don't purée it: you want the children to be able to see what they are eating. Most of the lentils will naturally fall to the bottom, so I just stir them in at the end.

Child with Adult: Taste the soup, then add enough salt and pepper to taste. Dipping into the spice combination, ask the children to add more spice to taste, and let them ream the lime and squeeze the juice in. Mix, and give them a ladle to put about a cup of soup carefully into each bowl. Ask them to sprinkle on the cilantro or parsley, and serve.

Note: Your children can make the soup their own by substituting chickpeas, sweet potatoes, red or yellow potatoes, zucchini, or any vegetables they like. Whatever you or they decide to do, the soup will be delicious.

SUKKOT

Sukkot Stuffed Vegetables 85
Children's Cholent: A Veggie-Bean Stew 88
Golden Harvest Tzimmes 90
Grandma's Seven Species Granola 91
Veggie Quiche 94
Pasta with Pesto and Green Beans 95
Eggplant Gratin 98
Zucchini Bread 99

Sukkot Harvest Menu

Chicken Schnitzel Tenders*

Sukkot Stuffed Vegetables*

Leafy Green Salad

Zucchini Bread*

Sukkot Sabbath Lunch

Children's Cholent: A Veggie-Bean Stew*

Pasta with Pesto and Green Beans*

Australian Carrot Dip*

Pita Bread*

Aunt Lisl's Butter Cookies* with Fruit

SUKKOT

The fall holiday of Sukkot has two stories to inform its observance. The first commemorates the Jews' wandering in the wilderness for forty years after fleeing Egypt; the second relates to the harvest time, when we lived in *sukkot* (booths or little huts) in the fields and vineyards. For the eight days of the Sukkot festival, foods are served in the fragile *sukkah* with three sides and an open top to let the sky show through, decorated with seasonal fruits and vegetables. Thus, it's a good time to think in terms of one-dish meals.

Our family's first *sukkah* was made of bamboo poles from a neighbor's hedge. We placed them on a rickety wood frame, which we hammered together and set on our deck. A *sukkah* must have at least three walls; the outside walls of the house can be used as the fourth. It can be set on a deck open to the sky or in a backyard. Whatever material is used should be strong enough to withstand normal winds but still fragile. The first year, we used colorful sheets as walls.

As our children grew older, the entire neighborhood joined us for our *sukkah* raising. The booth was made in our backyard, of wood beams that braced it to withstand the wind. The bamboo poles formed the roof. Cornstalks, tied down with garbage-bag twists, were the walls and see-through ceiling. A staple gun helped attach the cards, paper rings, and children's pictures as decorations. The children, from both regular and religious schools, helped decorate the *sukkah,* stringing popcorn, string beans, cranberries, and any leftover foods from our almost-dormant garden. Donuts and cider were served to the builders. Occasionally, we ate meals in our *sukkah,* but, honestly, for us, the most fun of all was just building it. Observant Jews eat all their meals there; some people even sleep in their *sukkot.*

The following blessing is said when you enter and sit down in the *sukkah:*

Baruch atah Adonai Eloheinu melech ha-olam asher kidshanu b'mitzvotav ve-tzivanu leishev ba-sukkah.

Blessed art Thou, Adonai, our God, Sovereign of the universe, who hast sanctified us with Thy commandments and commanded us to dwell in the sukkah.

The lulav (literally, palm branch) and the etrog (the fragrant yellow fruit of the citron) are also symbols of Sukkot. The lulav is a bouquet or small holder made with branches of willow, strands of green myrtle, and slender leaves of palm, bound together. To keep the lulav fresh throughout the holiday, it is taken apart at the end of each day and the branches stored in wet newspaper in the refrigerator. It is reassembled each morning. Be sure to save the lulav for Passover, when it can be used in place of the feather to search for *chametz* (page 161). For very observant Jews the etrog is kept in a special box or container, protected so that the stem of the fruit will not come off as the fruit, mentioned in the Bible, must have certain characteristics to be in a perfect state for the blessing. After the holiday, you can stick cloves in the etrog, just as you did when you "embalmed" an apple (page 43), and use it for Havdalah the rest of the year.

When you hold the lulav and the etrog, pointing and shaking them slowly in all four directions and up and down to show that God is everywhere, as are His blessings, the following prayer is said:

Baruch atah Adonai Eloheinu melech ha-olam asher kidshanu b'mitzvotav ve-tzivanu al netilat lulav.

Blessed art Thou, Adonai, our God, Sovereign of the universe, who has sanctified us with Your commandments and commanded us about the waving of the lulav.

Since Sukkot often falls during the harvest of our backyard garden, we try to make lots of stuffed vegetable and fruit dishes. If we are lucky, we still have fresh raspberries, which we pop right into our mouths from the bush. Finally, Sukkot also emphasizes welcoming guests—including the memory of our ancestors—into our *sukkah*. It is a good opportunity to share a meal with friends or extended family.

SUKKOT STUFFED VEGETABLES

Serves 6

INGREDIENTS

- 6 medium-size vegetables, according to the children's tastes: zucchini, yellow squash, bell peppers, tomatoes, onions, large carrots, etc.
- 2 cups boiling water
- 1 cup uncooked rice or orzo pasta
- 1 teaspoon salt
- 1 onion
- 2 tablespoons vegetable oil
- 1 cup frozen corn
- 1 cup frozen peas and carrots
- 2 tablespoons currants or raisins
- Freshly ground black pepper to taste
- ¼ teaspoon ground nutmeg
- ¼ teaspoon ground cinnamon
- 2 teaspoons fresh mint leaves or 1 teaspoon dried
- 2 tablespoons chopped fresh parsley
- 1 cup canned stewed tomatoes

EQUIPMENT

- Measuring cups
- Measuring spoons
- Apple corer
- 1½-quart pot with lid
- Knife
- Frying pan
- 4 small bowls
- Spoon
- Toothpicks
- Large heat-resistant casserole with cover

When I lived in Jerusalem, there was a tiny restaurant near the Eden Movie Theater called Michel Cohen's that served—all year long—stuffed zucchini, eggplant, figs, carrots, green peppers, potatoes, onions, Jerusalem artichokes, tomatoes, even prunes. Stuffed cabbage, grape leaves, and strudel are traditional for the harvest festival of Sukkot, symbolizing the wish for fullness in the year to come. Let your imagination and taste guide you with this recipe.

Child: Wash the vegetables well. For most vegetables all you need is a knife but for zucchinis, with an apple corer, carefully tunnel out holes big enough to put in your filling. Be sure not to cut through the bottom.

Child: Put the rice or pasta and the salt in the boiling water. Cover, lower the heat, and simmer for 20 minutes. Don't open the pot, or the rice won't cook right.

Child with Adult: Chop the onion very finely, and sauté it in the oil, unless you think onions are yucky. But you would be surprised how many things taste really good with onions in them. »

Sukkot Stuffed Vegetables continued »

Child with Adult: Place the corn in one bowl, the peas and carrots in another, the cooked rice in a third, and the currants, pepper, spices, and herbs in a fourth.

Child: Stuff whatever fillings each person particularly likes into the vegetables, leaving a slight amount of space for expansion at the top. Mark each person's vegetable with toothpicks, either different-colored ones or different numbers of toothpicks.

Child: Place the vegetables in a casserole large enough to hold them all.

Adult: Cover with the tomatoes, and add water to cover. Simmer, covered, for about 30 minutes, or until the vegetables show only the slightest resistance when pierced with the point of a sharp knife.

CHILDREN'S CHOLENT: A VEGGIE-BEAN STEW

Serves at least 10

INGREDIENTS

1 cup dried lima or kidney beans

2 large onions

2 cloves garlic

⅔ cup plus 2 tablespoons vegetable oil

6 carrots (about 1 pound)

6 sweet potatoes, peeled (about 3 pounds)

1 eggplant, 3 zucchini, or 3 yellow squash

1 cup pearl barley

4 tablespoons date molasses or honey

2 tablespoons baharat spice mixture

1 tablespoon salt, plus more as needed

Freshly ground black pepper to taste

2 teaspoons hot or sweet paprika

4 to 6 dates

6 eggs in their shells

6 medium potatoes (about 1½ pounds)

2 cups unbleached all-purpose flour

1 tablespoon baking powder

EQUIPMENT

Bowl

Measuring cups

Measuring spoons

Large ovenproof casserole with lid

Strainer or colander

Teakettle

When my grandchildren's great-grandmother was a little girl in Poland, her favorite Sabbath dish was cholent, the long-cooking stew put into the oven and sealed on Friday, before the Sabbath began, and then eaten on Saturday for lunch. Her favorite part of the dish was the thinly sliced potatoes her mother put on top. Today, during a period of history in which more and more young people rejoice in their Judaism, potluck dairy Shabbat luncheons are more and more common, and a volunteer often makes a cholent. It used to be that they were flavored with onion-soup mix, garlic powder, and onion flakes. No more. This generation includes instead a Middle Eastern flavor combination of baharat, a mixture of seven lucky spices that vary from cook to cook, but often include paprika, cinnamon, cumin, turmeric, nutmeg, allspice, cardamom, ginger, black pepper, and coriander; the name comes from the word *bahar,* a term for spices in both Arabic and Hebrew. Choose seven of your favorite spices and create your very own spice combination.

It is great fun for children to help make a cholent, either vegetarian, like this one, or with 3 pounds of chuck roast, whiffing the aroma as it cooks all night long. Start before the beginning of Shabbat and watch the result; make sure your children are present when you open the cover, so they can see the steam and sniff the wonderful scent.

Let the Sabbath during Sukkot be the first time of the year you serve cholent—a one-dish meal is very easy to carry out to the *sukkah.* You can also make this for festive occasions as I did for a kids' Hanukkah celebration, starting early in the morning. Everyone loved it.

Child: The night before starting to prepare the cholent, put the lima or kidney beans in a bowl and cover them with water. Let them soak overnight and wake up to see how the beans have expanded.

Adult with Child: The next day, at least 2 hours before the beginning of Shabbat, cut the onions and the garlic separately with a paring knife. First, sauté the onions in the bottom of a large casserole in 2 tablespoons of the oil, and then add the garlic, cooking until the onions are translucent. The reason we do this is that sometimes the garlic burns if cooked as long as the onions.

Child with Adult: Cut each carrot into three pieces, the sweet potatoes in half, and the eggplant, zucchini, or yellow squash into small chunks, about 2 inches in diameter. Put them all in the casserole with the barley and date molasses or honey, baharat, salt and pepper, paprika, dates, and the eggs in their shells.

Child: Drain the beans. Add them to the casserole.

Child with Adult: Cover the vegetables with about 10 cups of water and bring to a boil.

Child: As the cholent is heating, carefully slice and peel the potatoes, and layer them over the top of all the vegetables.

Child with Adult: Preheat the oven and make a dough from the remaining ⅔ cup vegetable oil, the flour, the baking powder, 1 teaspoon salt or to taste, and about 4 tablespoons of ice water. This should make a soft, malleable dough. Let the dough rest for a few minutes, then roll out to a few inches wider than the pot you are using and spread the dough all around the rim of the casserole, like putty. Put on the lid, sticking it to the dough to make sure no air gets in during cooking. Bake in a 250 degree oven for 8 to 12 hours. When it is time for lunch, open and eat!

Note: Add 3 pounds of chunks of chuck roast if you want meat in your cholent.

GOLDEN HARVEST TZIMMES

Serves 8

INGREDIENTS

- 4 carrots
- 2 sweet potatoes or yams
- 2 pounds butternut squash (I love cheating with prepeeled and deseeded halves at the supermarket)
- 2 apples
- ¼ cup raisins
- ½ cup orange juice
- ¼ cup brown sugar
- 1 teaspoon ground cinnamon
- ¼ cup (½ stick) salted butter or vegan spread

EQUIPMENT

- Measuring cups
- Measuring spoons
- Paring knife or vegetable peeler
- Large pot with lid
- Apple corer
- Ovenproof casserole or foil baking cups

One of the first Yiddish words I ever learned was *tzimmes.* "Don't make a *tzimmes* out of that!" scolded my grandmother. She meant not to make a big deal out of a small thing. A *tzimmes* is literally a mixture of vegetables and fruit and sometimes meat, a "big deal" casserole. Whatever the other ingredients (sometimes pineapple, prunes, even puréed mango in Mexico), there is one constant ingredient—carrots. Use your imagination on this one. Make it with dates, prunes, pumpkin—whatever foods your children like. When my son, David, was four years old, he created a face for a *tzimmes:* the head was made of slices of sweet potato, the eyes were carrots, the nose was an apple, and the mouth a slice of Hubbard squash.

Child: Peel the carrots, sweet potatoes or yams, and squash.

Adult with Child: Using a sharp knife, cut the vegetables in half or, if large, into quarters; show the children how to be careful and keep their fingers from getting cut. If using a whole squash, scoop the seeds and save them to roast for a snack!

Adult: Boil the carrots, sweet potatoes or yams, and squash in about ¾ quart salted water, covered, for 20 minutes, or until tender. Drain, saving a few cups of the liquid.

Child: When the vegetables are cool, cut them into circles, or any shape the children want.

Child: Core the apples and slice them into circles, about ¼-inch thick.

Adult: Preheat the oven to 400 degrees, and grease an oblong or circular casserole.

Child: Decorate the bottom of the casserole with the vegetables and then the apples. Sprinkle everything with the raisins. Pour the orange juice over it. Sprinkle with the brown sugar and cinnamon, and dot with the butter or vegan spread.

Adult: Bake for 25 minutes, or until well-browned. Serve, respecting whatever creations your children have made, but at least topping each portion with an apple circle.

GRANDMA'S SEVEN SPECIES GRANOLA

Makes about 8 cups

INGREDIENTS

¾ cup coarse bulgar

4 cups old-fashioned rolled oats

1½ cups almonds

¼ cup date molasses, or to taste

¼ cup extra-virgin olive oil

½ cup raisins or ½ cup dried figs, chopped

¾ cup shredded dried unsweetened coconut flakes

Pomegranate seeds, for serving

Yogurt, for serving

EQUIPMENT

Medium mixing bowl

Saucepan

Measuring cup

Parchment paper

Colander

Very large mixing bowl

Large wooden spoon

1 or 2 baking sheets

Containers, to store the granola

. . . a land of wheat and barley, and vines and fig-trees and pomegranates; a land of olive-trees and honey; a land wherein thou shalt eat bread without scarceness, thou shalt not lack any thing in it; a land whose stones are iron, and out of whose hills thou mayest dig brass.

—DEUTERONOMY 8:8–9

This is a great way to experience the flavors of the Biblical foods that our ancestors ate as children. In fact, a Biblical precursor of our modern granola is kolo, an Ethiopian and Yemenite snack for children made of barley and nuts that dates back to the Talmudic period. You can find modern-day kolo in Ethiopian stores or follow the recipe in *My Life in Recipes*.

I like to make large quantities of this seven-species granola for breakfast, and noticed that Alma and Aviv enjoyed making it with me when they were just two years old. It is very easy, and they loved just throwing all these ingredients into a large bowl and moving the ingredients around with their hands. What makes this very special is that, after baking it for 20 minutes, we turn off the oven and leave it overnight to cool. The result is a crispy and clumpy texture that we all love. It is delightful mixed with fresh berries, bananas, yogurt, and, of course, the seventh species from the land of Israel and Mesopotamia, pomegranate seeds. Although oats are not one of the seven Biblical species, they are as old as the Bible, and so is coconut, which originated in Southeast Asia.

Adult with Child: Combine the bulgar with 1½ cups water in a saucepan, and bring to a boil. Simmer for at least 12 minutes, until the bulgar is tender. Drain the bulgar in a colander.

Adult: Preheat the oven to 350 degrees, and help the children cover the baking sheets with parchment. »

Grandma's Seven Species Granola continued »

Child with Adult: Using a super-large mixing bowl, guide the children to measure out the oats and almonds. Add the cooked bulgar. Have them drizzle on the date molasses using more or less to taste and the olive oil, then mix very well with a big wooden spoon—they'll love doing this. Use the big spoon or your hands to scoop up the mixture and transfer it to the baking sheet(s). Pat down the granola into a thin layer.

Adult: Carefully put the baking sheet(s) into the oven and bake for 20 minutes, rotating the sheet(s) halfway through.

Child: Turn off the oven, and leave the granola for 2 hours or as long as overnight. This step is essential to achieve crispy clumps. Then remove it from the oven, and scatter on the raisins or chopped figs and the coconut.

Adult with Child: Carefully ladle the granola into tins or jars for storage. Serve it with other fresh foods of your liking. To keep it Biblical, serve it topped with pomegranate seeds and yogurt.

VEGGIE QUICHE

Makes 1 quiche, serving 6 to 8

INGREDIENTS

CRUST

- One 9-inch prepared crust
- or
- ½ cup (1 stick) unsalted butter or vegan spread
- 1¼ cups unbleached all-purpose flour
- Pinch of salt
- 2 tablespoons cold water

FILLING

- 4 large eggs
- 1½ cups milk
- Salt and freshly ground black pepper to taste
- Ground nutmeg, to taste
- ½ cup shredded sharp hard cheese, like cheddar or Gruyère
- 2 cups chopped zucchini, yellow squash, blanched broccoli, or most any vegetable

EQUIPMENT

- Food processor
- Measuring cups
- Measuring spoons
- Plastic wrap
- Rolling pin
- 9-inch deep-dish pie pan
- Mixing bowl
- Fork or wire whisk
- Mixing spoon

This is a great main dish for leftover vegetables and cheese. I have learned through the years that if children own a dish they will be more likely to eat it. Once you've figured out the main formula for making quiche, the rest is easy. You can do this with all kinds of vegetables. I have made it with broccoli and spinach. Buy a frozen prepared crust or make your own, which is much easier to do than many people realize, takes less time than going to the supermarket, and is much more fun.

TO MAKE THE CRUST

Adult with Child: Using a food processor, combine the butter or vegan spread, flour, and salt. Spin or blend well until the dough is crumbly, slowly adding the cold water. When a soft ball forms, wrap it in plastic wrap and refrigerate it for about 1 hour, or until firm.

Adult: Preheat the oven to 400 degrees.

Adult with Child: On a lightly floured surface, roll the dough into a circle about ⅛ inch thick. Don't bear down on the rolling pin. Just move it from the center away from you, easily. It will flatten more gently that way. When the dough is ⅛ inch thick, lay it in the bottom and up the sides of a 9-inch deep-dish pie pan, shaping it to fit the pan. Pinch the edges to trim any extra dough. Prick the bottom of the dough a few times with the tines of a fork, and bake it for 10 minutes, or until it's golden brown.

TO MAKE THE FILLING

Child: In a mixing bowl, beat the eggs well. Add the milk, salt, pepper, nutmeg, and cheese. Mix well. Add the vegetables, and mix well again.

Adult with Child: Carefully pour the mixture into the pie pan lined with either your homemade crust or the prepared one. Lower the heat to 375 degrees, and bake for 30 minutes, or until the custard is set. Slice it, and serve it with a salad.

PASTA WITH PESTO AND GREEN BEANS

Serves 4 to 6

INGREDIENTS

- ¼ cup pine nuts, walnuts, or almonds
- ¼ cup extra-virgin olive oil
- 2 cups packed fresh basil leaves
- 2 cloves garlic, minced
- 1 teaspoon salt, or to taste
- 4 cups chopped fresh green beans or other chopped vegetables
- ½ pound trofie pasta, or the pasta of your choice
- ¾ cup freshly grated Parmesan cheese
- Freshly ground black pepper to taste
- 12 cherry tomatoes

EQUIPMENT

- Toaster oven
- Measuring cups
- Measuring spoons
- Food processor, or mortar and pestle
- Large pot with a lid
- Knife
- Metal colander or strainer
- Serving bowl

Pesto with pasta is still a favorite with my children, and now with my grandchildren. I think it is particularly appropriate during Sukkot, when green beans are still being harvested in our garden and the weather is still warm. Snipping beans is a great occupation, even in front of the television. Or you can add or substitute zucchini, yellow squash, eggplant, or any other vegetable from your garden or the supermarket.

Let the children decide which vegetables and which pasta shape to use. Use your kids' favorite pasta—my grandchildren's is penne—but, to really have fun, try authentic trofie (pronounced tro-fee-eh) online, the true pasta for pesto. It has an elongated and curled shape, wrapping around itself. The first time I made pesto with trofie for my grandchildren, Alma and Aviv said they felt very grown up indeed.

When my friend the chef Nancy Silverton gave me the pesto recipe from her restaurant Mozza in Los Angeles, I found it was surprisingly similar to my own. She makes it with her grandson Ike, who is about the same age as my twins. In Liguria, the Italian Riviera, they say that the best basil grows only near the sea—but use what you have. And from my daughter Daniela, who makes pesto almost once a week, I learned to steam the vegetables in a metal colander on top of the pasta, and to use one of many nut substitutes for the so-expensive pine nuts. She also sneaks into the pesto nettle, parsley, chard, or spinach, which kids will eat with pasta but not alone on a plate. It is incredibly flexible, and a great way to add more vegetables to dinner.

Adult with Child: Toast the pine nuts, walnuts, or almonds in a toaster oven at 350 degrees for about 5 minutes, watching carefully to make sure the nuts don't burn.

Adult with Child: Put the olive oil and the basil in a mortar and pestle or a food processor with the sharp blade. Add the garlic, toasted nuts, and salt, and process or pound until the mixture is broken up and the texture is crunchy. It will take longer, but the kids will have lots of fun doing this if you choose to use the mortar and pestle. After all, "pesto" means "pounded" or "crushed" in Italian, and that is what you are doing with the basil leaves, the nuts, and the garlic. »

Pasta with Pesto and Green Beans continued »

Adult: Fill a large pot with cold water and a little more salt. Cover the pot, and bring the water to a boil.

Child: While the water is coming to a boil, put the green beans in the colander or strainer, and wash them under cold water. Then find a comfortable spot to sit or stand, and carefully break off both pointed ends of each green bean; this is called "snipping the beans." Put the beans back in the colander.

Adult with Child: Pour the pasta into the water, and set the colander full of beans on the pot, to steam. Once the beans are cooked to your liking, set them aside. Cook the pasta until it's al dente, then drain.

Adult: Toss the pesto with the drained pasta, the green beans, and the cheese. Adjust to taste, adding more cheese, basil, or oil as needed. Season with freshly grated pepper, and garnish with cherry tomatoes. Serve immediately or at room temperature.

CBG

EGGPLANT GRATIN

Serves about 8

INGREDIENTS

¾ cup olive oil

4 plump eggplants or zucchini (4 pounds total)

Salt and freshly ground black pepper, to taste

4 cloves garlic, peeled

One 28-ounce can San Marzano crushed tomatoes

1 cup chopped fresh oregano, basil, or preferably a mix, with chives and mint, too

10 ounces goat cheese

1 cup heavy cream or yogurt

⅓ cup freshly grated Parmesan cheese

EQUIPMENT

2 baking sheets

Parchment paper

Brush

9-by-13-inch casserole

Knife

2 medium bowls

Measuring spoons

Measuring cup

Spoons

When I was trying to think of an eggplant dish to feature, I chose this one, which my husband and I tasted in North Haven, Maine, when we went on a surprise boat trip with friends from Camden to a farm dinner. Since I am a big eggplant enthusiast, this dish is at the top of my list—a real crowd pleaser at the potlucks to which I have brought it. In fact, once I brought it to a potluck at my children's school when Julia Child accompanied me. If I don't have enough eggplant at the house, or if children don't like eggplant, I switch to zucchini or yellow squash.

Adult with Child: Preheat the oven to 425 degrees, cover two baking sheets with parchment paper, and brush a casserole with olive oil.

Adult with Child: Carefully slice the eggplants or zucchini into rounds ⅓ inch thick, and put them on the baking sheets. Brush olive oil over them, and sprinkle them with salt and pepper. Bake for about 20 minutes, rotating the sheets halfway through.

Adult: While the eggplant is cooking, chop the garlic and mix it with 3 cups of the tomatoes in one bowl.

Child: Then mix the herbs and goat cheese with the heavy cream or yogurt in another bowl, and set it aside.

Adult with Child: Spoon a third of the tomato sauce into the casserole, making sure it covers the bottom. Then add a third of the eggplant in a single layer. Top with dollops of the herb-goat-cheese mixture. Don't worry, these dollops will spread. Repeat twice, ending with dollops of the cheese. Sprinkle with the Parmesan cheese, lower the oven to 375 degrees, bake for about 20 minutes, or until bubbly, and serve.

ZUCCHINI BREAD

Makes 2 small loaves or 1 large loaf

INGREDIENTS

- 3 large eggs
- 1½ cups sugar
- 1 cup vegetable oil
- 3 teaspoons vanilla extract
- 2 medium zucchini
- 3 cups unbleached all-purpose flour
- 1 teaspoon salt
- 1 teaspoon baking soda
- ¼ teaspoon baking powder
- 3 teaspoons ground cinnamon
- ½ teaspoon ground nutmeg
- 1 cup coarsely chopped walnuts, chocolate chips, or coconut flakes, or a mix

EQUIPMENT

- Measuring cups
- Measuring spoons
- Two mixing bowls
- Fork or wire whisk
- Grater or food processor
- Spoon
- Two 8-by-5-inch loaf pans
- Rubber scraper
- Cooling rack

This variation on the late James Beard's recipe has been a staple for me ever since I picked the first zucchini from our garden. And it's one of my children's and grandchildren's favorites. Although zucchini bread has been around forever, I believe that this recipe put it on the national map before the Internet made it a ubiquitous summer treat. We eat it all year long; a slice of it will even go well at Hanukkah with some fruit cup or compote. »

Zucchini Bread continued »

Child: Beat the eggs with a fork or wire whisk in a mixing bowl until they're light and foamy. Add the sugar, oil, and vanilla, and mix gently but well.

Adult with Child: Grate the zucchini by hand, or show the child how to use the steel blade of a food processor. Add the zucchini to the egg mixture.

Adult: Preheat the oven to 350 degrees.

Child: Mix together the flour, salt, baking soda, baking powder, cinnamon, and nutmeg in a second bowl. Add this to the zucchini mixture. Stir until everything is well blended. Add the walnuts, chocolate chips, or coconut flakes, and pour the batter into the loaf pans, getting out any leftover batter with a rubber scraper.

Adult: Bake for 1 hour. Cool on a rack.

HANUKKAH

Aviv's Banana or Alma's Strawberry Pancakes 106

Potato Latkes 107

Applesauce 108

Vegan Chickpea Pancakes 109

Apple Latkes 110

East Coast Bread Furst Brownies from Washington, D.C. 113

West Coast Gluten-free Brownies from Valerie Confections in
Echo Park, Los Angeles 114

Ice Cream Cupcake Edible Menorah 115

Edible Dreidel 118

Aunt Lisl's Butter Cookies 120

Sufganiyot 122

Hanukkah Latke Party Menu

Potato Latkes*

Vegan Chickpea Pancakes*

Vegetable Latkes

Apple Latkes*

Applesauce*

Ice Cream Cupcake Edible Menorah*

Edible Dreidels*

Hanukkah Shabbat Dinner

Chicken Soup with Matzo Balls*

My Favorite Brisket

Potato Latkes*

Applesauce*

Sufganiyot*

HANUKKAH

"Can you guess, children, which is the best of all holidays? Hanukkah, of course . . . You eat pancakes every day," said the Yiddish writer Sholem Aleichem, best known by the musical *Fiddler on the Roof*, which was based on his stories. Who doesn't like potato latkes? These Russian potato pancakes were once a poor man's dish, cooked in goose fat to symbolize the miracle of Hanukkah. My husband, Allan, used to tell the story of the miracle more than two thousand years ago, of the weak conquering the mighty: the Maccabee brothers' defeat of the Seleucid King Antiochus's huge army, which was trying to make the Jews give up their religion. When the Temple was clean, the people wanted to light the hanukkiyah, called the Hanukkah menorah. There was only enough oil for one day, but by another miracle it burned for eight days. And so we celebrate Hanukkah to commemorate the rededication of the Temple in Jerusalem.

In the book of Exodus, there is an even earlier significance of using oil in a menorah during this darkest time of year. "You shall further instruct the Israelites to bring you clear oil of beaten olives for lighting, for kindling lamps regularly. Aaron and his sons shall set them up in the Tent of Meeting, outside the curtain which is over [the Ark of] the Pact, to burn from evening to morning before Adonai. It shall be a due from the Israelites for all time, throughout the ages." (Exodus 27:20–21)

Although Hanukkah, the Festival of Lights, is a relatively minor religious holiday, it has assumed major importance in our country. It comes right at Christmastime, but in our family, we do not try to compete with Christmas. I explain that everyone has a winter holiday to brighten up those cold days, and then, of course, we go into the traditions of Hanukkah.

In our house, we celebrate with our very close friends and their children. It is a joyful, fun-filled time, with presents for each child, dreidel spinning, cookie decorating, and a festive meal of pot roast, potato pancakes, applesauce, and Hanukkah cookies, which the children help prepare.

Makes about 16 pancakes

INGREDIENTS

1 cup unbleached all-purpose flour

1 cup cornmeal or johnnycake meal

1 tablespoon baking powder

1 tablespoon sugar

Pinch of salt

2 large eggs

6 tablespoons butter, melted, or vegetable oil

1 cup milk or buttermilk

1 teaspoon vanilla extract

1½ cups mashed bananas, sliced strawberries, or blueberries

Maple syrup, for serving

EQUIPMENT

¼ cup ladle

Large heavy skillet or griddle

2 mixing bowls, large and medium

Wooden spoon

Pancake flipper

AVIV'S BANANA OR ALMA'S STRAWBERRY PANCAKES

My children, and now my grandchildren, adore pancakes, and because I grew up in Rhode Island, we all like to give them a little johnnycake texture with cornmeal. Aviv insists on adding bananas, of which I have many in the freezer, peeled and tossed into plastic bags, and Alma likes strawberries. You can add either one, or both, or use blueberries, which I also like! Just remember: when you're making pancakes, don't overmix. Be gentle with your batter. Pancakes are a proper way to start the morning on one of the days of Hanukkah. After all, an American pancake is like a sweet latke.

Adult with Child: Mix the flour, cornmeal or johnnycake meal, baking powder, sugar, and salt in a large bowl.

Using a smaller bowl, beat the eggs with 4 tablespoons of the butter or oil, the milk or buttermilk, and the vanilla, and stir this into the dry ingredients, beating gently just to blend, adding more milk or buttermilk if too thick. Fold in the fruit you have chosen.

Adult: Add ½ tablespoon of butter or oil to the skillet or griddle for each round.

Child with Adult: Fill a small ladle with batter, about ¼ cup, and carefully spoon it into the pan. Cook the pancakes a few at a time until they bubble and start to get brown around the edges (and are not too juicy in the center, says Aviv), about 3 minutes. Then carefully flip them over, and cook the other side until golden. (Aviv and Alma got very good at flipping them into the air to turn them over!) Repeat to use all the batter, and serve them with maple syrup.

Note: If you do not cook on the Sabbath, make these another day and either freeze or refrigerate them, then heat them up in the already heated oven for Sabbath breakfast.

POTATO LATKES

Makes 24 to 36 latkes, depending on size

INGREDIENTS

- 6 large russet (baking) potatoes
- 1 large onion
- 3 large eggs, beaten
- 1 tablespoon salt
- ¼ teaspoon freshly ground black pepper
- ¾ cup matzo meal
- Vegetable oil, for frying

EQUIPMENT

- Vegetable peeler
- Pan of ice water
- Measuring cups
- Measuring spoons
- Food processor or hand grater
- Mixing bowl
- Spoon
- 10-inch frying pan
- Pancake turner
- Paper towels
- Baking sheet (optional)

To most American Jews, a potato latke equals Hanukkah. In this traditional recipe, you could also vary the potatoes by adding carrots, zucchini, and eggplant, as well as some mint. We know that applesauce or sour cream is the usual accompaniment, but why not try spooning yogurt and walnuts on top, or ask your children to suggest a favorite topping? Tzatziki (page 132) is always a good bet, too.

Child: Peel the potatoes, and put them in a pan of ice water to make sure they do not turn gray, or oxidize.

Adult with Child: This is a perfect way to teach your child how to use the food processor. Depending on the child's age, keep a good watch over him or her. Use the steel blade or the shredding blade to grate the potatoes and onion. Show the child how to use the "pulse" button, or turn the machine on and off frequently, so the vegetables don't turn into the soupy mess called a purée. Vegetables can also be grated by hand with an aluminum grater.

Child: In a bowl, mix together the grated potatoes and onion, beaten eggs, salt, and pepper. Stir in the matzo meal. Shape the batter into pancakes, about 4 or 5 inches wide and about ¼ inch thick, using 2 heaping tablespoons of mixture for each.

Adult with Child: Fry the latkes, a few at a time, in 1 to 2 tablespoons hot oil for 1½ minutes per side, or until golden. Add additional oil as necessary. Drain them on paper towels. Serve them hot with applesauce (recipe follows), or the topping of your choice.

Note: If desired, fry the latkes ahead of time and drain them on paper towels for 1 to 2 hours at room temperature. Reheat them on an ungreased baking sheet in a 350 degree oven for 8 to 10 minutes. You can also freeze the cooked latkes to store them. Reheat them in a 350 degree oven for about 15 minutes.

APPLESAUCE

Makes 4 cups

INGREDIENTS

- 4 pounds flavorful baking apples, such as Honeycrisp, Fuji, Gala, or Jonagold, peeled and cored
- 1 lemon, including rind
- Handful of Red Hots, to taste, and for color
- ½ cup apple juice, cider, or water
- Honey or maple syrup, to taste (optional)

EQUIPMENT

- Measuring cup
- Knife
- Heavy pot with lid
- Wooden spoon
- Food mill
- Mixing bowl

This is a recipe with which our children love to improvise. Many, many years ago, I learned the trick of adding Red Hots to applesauce, from a friend of my mother's. They add color and give the applesauce a slight cinnamon zing of flavor.

Child with Adult: Roughly chop the apples and lemon into quarters. (No need to chop more finely—the goodness stays in.) Place them in a heavy pot with the Red Hots to taste. Add the apple juice, cider, or water.

Adult: Cover the pot, bring the liquid to a boil, and then simmer it over low heat, stirring occasionally to turn the apples and make sure they do not stick. You may want to add some more liquid. Cook about 20 minutes, or until the apples are soft. Let them cool slightly.

Child with Adult: Put the sauce through a food mill, and taste; add honey or maple syrup to taste if you want it sweeter (though I rarely do). Refrigerate it until you're ready to serve.

Makes about 12 pancakes

INGREDIENTS

- 1½ cups chickpea flour
- 1 teaspoon salt
- Freshly ground black pepper, to taste
- 1 bunch scallions or 1 small onion, chopped
- 2 tablespoons olive oil for sauteing and frying, plus more as needed
- 1 cup cooked or frozen corn
- 2 tablespoons chopped fresh parsley or dill

EQUIPMENT

- Measuring cups
- Medium saucepan
- Wooden spoon
- Cast-iron or other sturdy frying pan
- Baking sheet (12 by 15 inches)
- Parchment paper
- Spatula
- Instant-read thermometer
- Slotted spoon
- Plate lined with paper toweling

Note: This recipe has endless possibilities—instead of corn, add zucchini, chopped red pepper, carrots, spinach, Swiss chard, or sorrel.

VEGAN CHICKPEA PANCAKES

As mentioned before, chickpeas are the oldest protein in the Western world. Although potato latkes are the definitely the most popular kind, why not try vegan chickpea pancakes? They are far older than the beloved potato latkes or Polish apple latkes, both recipes that have followed Jews wherever they have gone. A version of this recipe without the corn (a New World crop) may have been the earliest latke; the Jews who went from ancient Israel to Rome may have brought this recipe to Sicily, a place where Jews settled after the destruction of the Second Temple in 70 C.E.

Child: In a medium saucepan, whisk together the chickpea flour, 3 cups of water, salt, and pepper.

Adult with Child: Place over medium-high heat and cook, stirring, until the mixture bubbles, becomes thick, and easily pulls away from the bottom and sides of the pan. This can take about 5 minutes. The mixture should be very thick, like a pudding, or else it will break apart when frying. If it's too thin, cook down a little more. Remove from the heat.

Adult with Child: Then sauté the scallions or onion in 2 tablespoons of the olive oil in the cast-iron skillet or other sturdy pan, mix them with the corn, and set the mixture aside. This will take 3 to 5 minutes.

Child: Stir the parsley or dill and the onion mixture into the chickpea mush, and pour this batter onto a parchment-lined baking sheet. Use a spatula to smooth the top to make it flat and even, about ¼ inch thick. Place the sheet in the refrigerator for an hour or so to cool and firm up.

Adult with Child: Just before you are ready to eat, add about an inch of olive oil to the cast-iron skillet. The temperature should read about 375 degrees, measuring with an instant-read thermometer. Cut the prepared mixture into squares, about 3 inches long. Lower them carefully into the oil without crowding the pan. Cook them in batches of 3 to 5, depending on the size of your pan, and make sure the heat returns to 375 each time for the next batch. Fry until the latkes are golden brown on one side, 2 to 3 minutes, then flip them and finish frying on the other side, another 2 to 3 minutes. Remove them with a slotted spoon, and let them drain on a paper-towel-lined plate before serving.

Makes 8 to 10 pancakes

INGREDIENTS

- 2 or 3 Granny Smith, Honeycrisp, or other flavorful apples, peeled
- 1 lemon
- 2 large eggs
- ½ teaspoon salt
- 1 teaspoon vanilla extract
- 1 tablespoon granulated sugar
- 2 tablespoons unbleached all-purpose flour
- 1 teaspoon baking powder
- ½ teaspoon ground cinnamon
- Dash of ground nutmeg
- 2 to 3 tablespoons unsalted butter
- Sour cream, Greek yogurt, or crème fraîche, for serving
- Berries, for serving
- Confectioners' sugar, for sprinkling

EQUIPMENT

- Box grater or food processor
- One or two mixing bowls
- Microplane
- Sharp knife
- Whisk
- Measuring spoons
- 12-inch heavy frying pan with ovenproof handle
- ¼-cup measuring cup
- Spatula
- Paper towels

APPLE LATKES

Hanukkah is a fine time to serve these at brunch with a dollop of Greek yogurt or sour cream on top. I am constantly amazed at just how far Jewish food travels: when I was working on the update for this book, my daughter Daniela told me that a relative of her Chilean friend posted a recipe online for apple latkes. When I contacted her, I realized it was a Polish recipe. Shortly afterward, Daniela, on a train going through Poland, tasted a similar apple pancake. You can also substitute stone fruits, like apricots, plums, or peaches—in the late spring, at Shavuot, or anytime.

Child with Adult: Using the large holes of a box grater, or using a food processor, grate the apples; squeeze them to remove some of the juice. Put the apples back in the food processor or transfer to a mixing bowl. Zest the lemon with a Microplane; then cut the lemon into two pieces with a sharp knife, and squeeze the juice of one half over the grated apples.

Child: In another bowl, carefully break and whisk the eggs; stir in the salt, vanilla, granulated sugar, flour, baking powder, cinnamon, and nutmeg. Do not overbeat. Then fold in the apples.

Child with Adult: Heat the frying pan, and swirl the butter around its surface. Then, using a ¼-cup measure, spread some batter to make one 3- or 4-inch pancake. Repeat, filling the skillet with no more than four pancakes at a time, and cook them on one side for 3 to 4 minutes, until golden and bubbling and brown around the edges. Flip with a spatula, and cook until golden on the other side. Drain them on paper towels, and serve them with a dollop of sour cream, Greek yogurt, or crème fraîche, fresh berries, and a sprinkle of confectioners' sugar.

Note: You can also substitute all kinds of berries or even chocolate chips for the apples. Mmm good!

EAST AND WEST BROWNIES

When my children were growing up, they loved visiting my aunt Lisl's daughter-in-law Dorothy the way I liked visiting Aunt Lisl. Dorothy invariably made her brownies for them.

Dorothy is no longer with us, and it is a different time. When my grandchildren visit me in Washington, I walk them up to my friend Mark Furstenberg's kid-friendly bakery, Bread Furst. There they and I have the deliciously rich brownies. With trepidation I asked for the recipe which Cecile Mouthan, a baker at the store, gave me. I divided it by thirty-two and omitted the espresso, and now we have a brownie recipe for, I believe, a generation of more sophisticated palates.

When I told my daughter Daniela that I was putting these East Coast brownies in the book, she reminded me of the deliciousness of the West Coast brownies from Valerie Echo Park in Los Angeles. Daniela had them at her wedding and I cut them in half as treats for my grandchildren when they come home from school. One day, Valerie Gordon, the owner, was in the store when we were and urged me to include what are now her gluten-free brownies. They can be made gluten free with buckwheat or regular with all-purpose flour. So, not wanting to consult with Solomon and having to choose a recipe, I have included both. »

EAST COAST BREAD FURST BROWNIES FROM WASHINGTON, D.C.

Makes about 18

INGREDIENTS

- 1½ sticks (1½ cups) unsalted butter or vegan spread
- 1½ cups sugar
- 1 cup unsweetened good-quality cocoa powder
- ½ teaspoon salt
- 4 large eggs
- 1 teaspoon vanilla extract
- ⅔ cup unbleached all-purpose flour
- 4 ounces 70% chocolate chunks or bittersweet chips

EQUIPMENT

- One 9-by-9-inch baking pan
- Knife
- Measuring cups
- Measuring spoons
- Mixing bowls
- Spatula or wooden spoon
- Fork or wire whisk
- Rubber scraper

Adult with Child: Preheat the oven to 325 degrees. Grease the baking pan with some of the butter or vegan spread, and then melt the rest in a saucepan or the microwave and let cool a bit.

Child: Pour the melted butter or vegan spread into a large bowl and stir in the sugar and cocoa powder with a spatula or a wooden spoon. Mix until smooth. Then add the salt, eggs, and vanilla. Carefully stir in the flour and the chocolate chunks or chips. (I purposely added a few chunks or chips to this measurement, knowing the kids will nibble a few!)

Adult with Child: Pour the brownie mixture into the prepared baking pan and bake for 25 to 30 minutes or until almost set. You want it to be a bit fudgy. Cool slightly and cut into squares.

WEST COAST GLUTEN-FREE BROWNIES FROM VALERIE CONFECTIONS IN ECHO PARK, LOS ANGELES

Makes 12 to 16

INGREDIENTS

1½ sticks (12 tablespoons) unsalted butter

3 ounces 99% unsweetened chocolate, chopped

1 cup (7 ounces) granulated sugar

½ cup (3 ounces) light-brown sugar

3 large eggs

¾ cup (3.75 ounces) buckwheat or all-purpose flour

1 teaspoon vanilla bean paste or vanilla extract

1 teaspoon salt

EQUIPMENT

One 9-by-9-inch baking pan

Knife

Measuring cups

Measuring spoons

Double boiler

Mixing bowls

Spatula or wooden spoon

Fork or wire whisk

Rubber scraper

Adult: Heat the oven to 350 degrees and grease the bottom and sides of a square pan with a teaspoon or so of the butter.

Adult with Child: Melt the rest of the butter and the chopped chocolate in the top of a double boiler or in a microwave, stirring occasionally, until they are melted and mixed. Stir both sugars into the chocolate mixture with a wooden spoon. Cool slightly and mix in the eggs one at a time. Add the buckwheat or all-purpose flour, vanilla, and salt, and stir until thoroughly combined.

Adult with Child: Spread the batter into the prepared baking pan and bake for about 30 minutes, until a crust forms and the center appears almost dry. Check the brownies with a toothpick—small crumbs should adhere when you pull it out. Let the brownies cool in the pan for at least 10 minutes on a cooling rack before cutting with a sharp knife.

Makes at least 12 cupcakes, 9 to make your menorah and a few extra to enjoy right away

INGREDIENTS

14 cream-filled chocolate sandwich cookies

3 tablespoons unsalted butter

1 pint chocolate cookie-dough or chocolate ice cream or frozen yogurt

Fresh raspberries, for garnish

EQUIPMENT

Food processor

Saucepan

12-cup muffin tin

Paper cupcake liners

Large spoon

Hanukkah candles

Aluminum foil

ICE CREAM CUPCAKE EDIBLE MENORAH

The menorah is the most meaningful symbol of Hanukkah. Artistic Jews throughout the world have created their own versions. I liked to take our children to local Jewish gift shops, synagogues, and museums to see the different renditions. We spent one Hanukkah in Jerusalem delighting in menorahs in windows.

For each of the eight nights of Hanukkah, an additional candle is inserted, from right to left, and lit by the *shammas,* or helper candle, from left to right, until the eight-candle menorah is aglow. We place our menorahs on a flameproof tray in our front window. If your children do not want to make their own menorah out of clay, let them make the following edible one.

Making your own menorah is one of the great pleasures of celebrating Hanukkah. Menorahs can come in all different shapes, made from nearly any materials, as long as each candle is kept separate and distinct from the others and they are in one line, with the *shammas* raised. These candle cupcakes can be arranged together in nearly any shape—a circle, a square, a straight line, or whatever you can imagine—to form a different and deliciously edible menorah.

Adult: To make the crust, whirl twelve of the cookies in a food processor until they're ground very fine. Melt the butter in a small saucepan or microwave, and mix well with the cookies.

Child: Put one paper cupcake liner in each muffin mold. Using your fingers, press about 1⁄14 of the cookie-butter mixture along the bottom and up the sides of each mold. Try to get the cookie mixture pressed in as smoothly and evenly as you can. Remove the ice cream or frozen yogurt from the freezer, let it soften slightly for a few minutes, and then spoon about 3⁄4 cup divided equally into the cookie molds, pressing down until smooth. Fill the molds with the ice cream or frozen yogurt.

Adult: Chill the filled tins in the freezer until the cupcakes hold together well, about 3 hours, or until you're ready to use them. »

Ice Cream Cupcake Edible Menorah continued »

Child: Insert a Hanukkah candle into the center of each cupcake. Refreeze until they're very solid in the tins, and wrap them well in aluminum foil. (You can even do this a week ahead.) When you're ready to make your menorah, remove the tins from the freezer, and carefully remove each cupcake, with its liner, from the tins. Arrange the menorah as you wish—in a row or a circle, but make sure to elevate the *shammas* by placing it on the remaining two sandwich cookies. Then immediately light the candles and say the blessings. Of course, this doesn't take the place of the real menorah. Be sure to blow out the candles before the ice cream gets soft!

Makes 1

INGREDIENTS

1 marshmallow
1 whole strawberry
1 Hershey's Kiss

EQUIPMENT

Toothpicks
Dull knife

EDIBLE DREIDEL

O dreidel, dreidel, dreidel
I made it out of clay
And when it's dry and ready
Then dreidel I shall play.

This is my favorite Hanukkah song. While you're eating sufganiyot (Israeli jelly doughnuts) and potato latkes, what better thing to do than play dreidel? It used to be a German gambling game. The rules are simple. The letters written on the four-sided top are *nun,* נ (nothing); *gimel,* ג (all); *heh,* ה (half); and *shin,* ש (add one item to the pot). Together, the letters mean "a great miracle happened here." Each person should start with about ten pennies, carob chips, nuts, raisins, M&M's, or stones. Each player puts one of these tokens in the pot and one in the center of the table or floor where they are playing. In turn, each person spins the dreidel, which is like a top. The face-up letter determines what he wins. When the pot is empty, each player adds one object to it. If an odd number of objects are in the pot, the *heh* person takes half plus one. When one person wins everything, the game is over.

When the children are tired of playing dreidel, they can make an edible one.

Child: Thread a toothpick through a marshmallow. Hold the strawberry with one hand and use a dull knife to cut it with your other hand into a 1-inch drum, then thread it onto the toothpick. (Strawberries are great fruit with which to practice cutting skills.) Add the kiss to the end. Eat it, don't spin it! Repeat to make more edible dreidels.

Makes 48 cookies or more, depending on your cookie cutters

INGREDIENTS

½ pound (2 sticks) unsalted butter or vegan spread, softened

¾ cup sugar

2 large eggs plus 1 egg, divided

Dash of salt

½ teaspoon vanilla extract

3½ cups unbleached all-purpose flour

1 egg yolk, plus chopped nuts and raisins
or
1 egg white, plus blue and white sprinkles

EQUIPMENT

Measuring cups

Measuring spoons

Mixing bowl or stand mixer

Wooden spoon

Rolling pin

2 baking sheets

Parchment paper

Cookie cutters or toothpicks

Pastry brush

Metal spatula

Cooling rack or flat plate

AUNT LISL'S BUTTER COOKIES

When I was a little girl, I always looked forward to visiting my aunt Lisl at Hanukkah. In her breezeway between the garage and the kitchen, in airtight containers, she stored the most delicious Bavarian butter cookies, which she made from the recipe she'd had since her childhood in Augsburg, Germany.

I delighted in decorating and then eating them, and taking some home with me.

Throughout my life, I have found that one of the best things about cooking with relatives is that it's a great time to ask for family stories. While we baked, Aunt Lisl told wonderful tales of my father's and her childhood before World War I and making these delicious cookies every December. Now I try to make the dough ahead of time, and when children enter my house we cut them out and bake them, then gobble them up for dessert.

Child: Using a bowl, or a stand mixer with a paddle, cream the butter or vegan spread and sugar. Then mix in the 2 eggs, salt, vanilla, and 3 cups of the flour. Let the dough rest for at least 30 minutes in the refrigerator.

Adult with Child: Toss the remaining ½ cup of flour on a board or over your rolling pin, and roll out the dough to ⅛ inch thick. Then preheat the oven to 350 degrees and line the baking sheets with parchment paper.

Child: You can either use cookie cutters, or use the point of a toothpick like a knife to cut out cookies in any shapes you want. Let your imagination run free: how about dreidels, Stars of David, candles with flames attached, or the four Hebrew letters on the dreidel?

Gently transfer the cookies onto the baking sheets. Then either brush them with egg yolk and sprinkle with nuts and raisins, or brush with egg white and decorate with blue and white sprinkles.

Adult: Bake for 10 to 12 minutes, or until the cookies are golden brown. Use a metal spatula to gently remove each cookie from the baking sheet to a cooling rack or flat plate.

SUFGANIYOT

Makes about 12

INGREDIENTS

- 1 scant tablespoon (1 package) active dry yeast
- 4 tablespoons sugar, plus more for rolling
- ¾ cup lukewarm milk or warm water*
- 2½ cups unbleached all-purpose flour
- Pinch of salt
- 1 teaspoon ground cinnamon
- 2 large eggs, separated
- 2 tablespoons (¼ stick) unsalted butter, coconut oil, or vegan spread, softened*
- Apricot, strawberry, or any other preserves
- Vegetable oil, for deep-frying

EQUIPMENT

- Measuring spoons
- Measuring cups
- Mixing bowls
- Spoon
- Sifter
- Clean dish towel
- Rolling pin
- Juice glass
- Deep-fryer or heavy pot
- Slotted spoon
- Paper towels
- Tiny spoon for filling the donuts

* If you're observing the dietary laws, use butter and milk if serving the sufganiyot at a milk meal, and water and coconut oil for a meat meal.

Most food traditions in Israel have been incorporated into the country's cuisine from immigrants' countries of origins. But *sufganiyot,* the popular jelly doughnut served at Hanukkah, is distinctly Israeli, created there and incorporated into the lexicon of Israeli cooking. The word comes from the Greek *sufgan* (puffed, fried, and spongy) and from the Hebrew *sofiget* (water) and *sofeg* (to blot).

When people first prepared these, they were made from two rounds of dough sandwiching jam, as I have done here. But now there are throwaway injectors you can get at Dollar Stores, as I did in Melbourne, Australia, when I made *sufganiyot* with the students in a Workmen's Circle, Sholem Aleichem school. You can first form the doughnuts in rounds, then fry them, and then inject them with your favorite jam. Be creative with this dessert, another representation of the miracle of Hanukkah, when the oil lasted for eight days instead of one.

Child: Mix together the yeast, 2 tablespoons of the sugar, and the milk or warm water. Let the mixture sit until it bubbles.

Child: Sift the flour, and mix it with the remaining 2 tablespoons sugar, the salt, cinnamon, egg yolks, and the yeast mixture.

Adult with Child: Knead the dough until it forms a ball. Add the butter, coconut oil, or vegan spread. Knead some more, until the butter is well absorbed. Cover the dough with a towel, and let it rise a few hours or overnight in the refrigerator.

Adult: Roll out the dough to a thickness of ⅛ inch.

Child, or Child with Adult: Cut out the dough into twenty-four rounds with a juice glass or any object about 2 inches in diameter. Take ½ teaspoon of preserves, and put it in the center of each of twelve rounds. Top with the other twelve rounds. Press down around the edges, then seal them by dipping your fingers in the egg whites, and then crimping all around the edges, using the egg white as a glue. Crimping with the thumb and second finger is easiest. Let the dough rise for about 30 minutes. As an alternative, you can roll the dough into twelve balls and inject the jam with a syringe.

Adult: Heat at least 2 inches of oil to about 375 degrees. Drop the doughnuts into the hot oil, about six at a time. Fry for a minute or two, then turn them to brown on the other side. Drain them on paper towels.

Child: Roll the doughnuts in sugar, and eat.

TU B'SHEVAT

Tu B'Shevat Challah 131
Tzatziki (Biblical Yogurt Dip) 132
Tree of Life Fruitful Salad 134
Peanut Butter–Stuffed Figs and Dates 135
Cherry Oatmeal Cookie Bars 137

Tu B'Shevat Dinner

Tu B'Shevat Challah*

Hummus*

Chicken Schnitzel Tenders*

Golden Harvest Tzimmes*

Peanut Butter–Stuffed Figs and Dates*

Tu B'Shevat Brunch

Tree of Life Fruitful Salad* with Tzatziki*

Shakshuka*

Bagels*

Cherry Oatmeal Cookie Bars*

TU B'SHEVAT

My strongest childhood memories of Tu B'Shevat are of the blue-and-white Jewish National Fund boxes into which I dutifully plunked my nickels and dimes to "plant trees in Israel." But not until I went to live in Jerusalem did I understand the real significance of the holiday, which is observed on the fifteenth day of the Hebrew month of Shevat, usually in January. During this month of heavy rains, which mark the end of winter and the beginning of spring, the sap in the fruit trees begins to rise. It is the Arbor Day of Israel. If it is not the right season for planting in your part of the world, start seedlings of parsley, lima beans, or sweet potatoes inside at Tu B'Shevat. The parsley will be ready to use on the Seder plate at Passover.

I had hardly learned my *alef-bet* at Ulpan Etzion in Jerusalem when I attended my first Tu B'Shevat tree-planting party in the seacoast town of Caesarea, which was founded in 30 BCE by Herod the Great. I often visited a family there at their weekend home near the Roman aqueduct on the beach, where I rode horses on the sand. The food was not fancy, but nuts and fruits abounded, to celebrate the "New Year of the Trees." It is customary at this time to eat as many as fifteen different kinds of fruits and nuts, such as carob, plums, pomegranates, pears, citrons, oranges, apples, dates, grapes, nuts, melons, and apricots. Carob pods (or carob chips made from the pods) are traditionally chewed in Israel at Tu B'Shevat—they taste like chocolate! While the guests were munching on dried fruits and nuts, all the time basking in the winter sunshine near the sea, we played a game. Someone named a fruit or nut, and we tried to find a Biblical passage mentioning its name. Then we discussed the symbolic meanings of the fruits and nuts. Here are a few:

Apple—symbol of a sweet year. But there are no apples in the Bible, not even in the Garden of Eden! Apples in the Bible stand for pomegranates, quinces, or apricots, any of them possibly the "apple" of Adam and Eve.

Apricot—the glowing splendor of God

Almond—blossoms of the almond, the first tree to bloom, stand for the swiftness of divine judgment.

Carob—the food of the poor. It represents humility and tastes like chocolate.

Pomegranate—because of its many seeds and bright red color, it's a symbol of fertility, peace, prosperity, and the many mitzvot that guide a Jewish life.

My children's Hebrew school held a Tu B'Shevat Seder, a Sephardic custom started in Spain and Middle Eastern countries. The children drank four cups of "wine" to symbolize the changes that nature undergoes in the four seasons. The lightest, apple juice, stands for the slumber that descends upon nature in the fall. Then, to symbolize the changes, the children drink orange, then cranberry, and finally dark grape juice, which evokes the awakening and blossoming of nature on Shevat 15.

At the Seder meal, the children tasted pieces of three different categories of fruits and nuts. They first picked up a new fruit of the season and then tasted from a variety of different fruits. The first category of fruit had a peel or a shell that isn't usually eaten: pistachio nuts, bananas, kiwis, oranges, avocados, almonds, pineapples, melons, and so on. The second had a pit inside that cannot be eaten: prunes, dates, apricots, plums, cherries, olives, and the like. The third category of fruit can be eaten entirely: strawberries, grapes, pears, figs, apples with the seeds, and raisins. Before the fruit is eaten, the following blessing is recited:

Baruch atah Adonai Eloheinu melech ha-olam, borei p'ri ha-etz.

Blessed art Thou, Adonai, our God, Sovereign of the universe, who createst the fruit of the tree.

At our home, we try to have a fruit-and-nut meal at Tu B'Shevat. You can even add nuts and raisins to your challah.

TU B'SHEVAT CHALLAH

Adult with Child: Follow the recipe on page 18 for challah. Just before the first rising, fold into the dough a cup of mixed chopped walnuts, dates, and raisins.

Makes 1 cup

INGREDIENTS

- 1 cucumber
- 1 cup yogurt
- 2 cloves garlic, mashed
- ½ cup chopped fresh mint
- Salt, to taste

EQUIPMENT

- Vegetable peeler
- Knife
- Measuring cups
- Food processor

TZATZIKI (BIBLICAL YOGURT DIP)

Tzatziki (Greek yogurt and cucumber dip) and raita (Indian yogurt-and-cucumber sauce with cumin and fresh cilantro) are similar to what I ate in Israel, a sauce including crisp cucumbers, yogurt, garlic, and fresh mint. Given the ubiquity of yogurt today, this is a healthful and tasty sort of Biblical yogurt dip; you can get your children to eat their fresh vegetables dipped into it, or serve it as a sauce for vegetables.

Child: Peel the cucumber, and cut it in half.

Adult with Child: Place the yogurt, the garlic, the cucumber, and the mint in a food processor, and pulse on and off. You do not want a purée. Add salt to taste, and chill the dip in the refrigerator for several hours. Drain off any liquid that accumulates, and serve.

TREE OF LIFE FRUITFUL SALAD

Serves 6

INGREDIENTS

1 orange, peeled, cut into slices, then halved

1 avocado, cut in half, carefully working around the pit, then cut across, then cut vertically and bend away the flesh

1 apple, peeled and diced

2 dates, pitted and sliced lengthwise

Seeds of ¼ pomegranate, or ¼ cup dried or fresh cranberries

¼ cup toasted pecans

½ head romaine lettuce, chopped

2 tablespoons tzatziki (preceding recipe)

EQUIPMENT

Measuring cup

Measuring spoon

Salad bowl

Salad spoons

This is a wonderfully creative recipe: fruits that you can craft into a tree of life, with avocado for the grass and round slices of orange for the sun. Remember that Adam and Eve in the Garden of Eden were forbidden to eat from the Tree of Knowledge—but this Tree of Life you can eat! Serve with hummus (page 26) or the Biblical yogurt dip tzatziki (preceding recipe).

Child: Combine the fruits, nuts, and lettuce in a salad bowl or craft it into a Tree of Life, using the dates as the tree trunk, the lettuce or avocado as the grass, and the orange sections as the sun. Just before serving, add the tzatziki. Toss fifteen times, in honor of the fifteen different kinds of fruits and nuts eaten on Shevat 15.

Makes 24

INGREDIENTS

12 dried figs

12 dates, pitted

Peanut butter

Grated coconut

EQUIPMENT

Knife

White paper candy cups

PEANUT BUTTER-STUFFED FIGS AND DATES

An old Jewish man in ancient Israel was planting a fig tree. The Roman Emperor passed by and said to him, "Why do you do that, old man? Surely, you will not live long enough to see it bear fruit."

"In that case," replied the man, "I will leave it for my son, as my father left the fruit of his labor for me."

The Emperor admired his spirit. "If you do live to see the figs on your tree ripen," he said, "let me know about it."

The old man lived to eat of the fruit and, remembering the Emperor's words, brought him a basket of figs. The Emperor was so pleased that he filled the old man's basket with gold.

A greedy woman who heard of the gift made her husband go to the Emperor, too. "He loves figs," she said, "and he will surely fill your basket with gold."

The man listened to his wife, brought the figs to the palace, and said, "These figs are for the Emperor. Empty my basket and fill it with gold!"

When the Emperor heard this, he ordered the guard to have all the people who passed by throw figs at the man. When the man finally escaped, he ran home and told his wife what had happened.

"Well," she said, "you are lucky. Think what would have happened if the figs had been coconuts!"

At the Sephardic Seder, figs stuffed with nuts and rolled in coconut are a common delicacy.

Adult with Child: Slit the center of each fig and date with a knife. Put about 1 tablespoon peanut butter in the center of each fruit. Close them up, and roll the stuffed fruit in grated coconut. Place them in small white paper cups.

CHERRY OATMEAL COOKIE BARS

Makes 16 small bars

INGREDIENTS

FOR THE CRUST AND CRUMBLE

- 1½ cups old-fashioned oats, whirled in a blender or a food processor into a coarse "flour"
- 1 cup old-fashioned oats
- ⅓ cup dark-brown sugar
- ½ teaspoon ground cinnamon
- ¼ teaspoon baking soda
- ¼ teaspoon salt
- ½ cup unsalted butter or vegan spread
- 1 teaspoon vanilla extract

FOR THE FILLING

- 3 cups fresh or frozen tart or sweet cherries
- 1 to 2 tablespoons maple syrup or light- or dark-brown sugar, depending on which cherries you use
- 1 tablespoon cornstarch (add more if necessary)
- ¼ teaspoon almond extract
- Pinch of salt
- ¼ cup roughly chopped or slivered almonds, toasted (optional)

When my friend Audrey Singer was in Israel, she tasted a delicious date bar with walnuts at a kibbutz, similar to one she gave me at her apartment, substituting cherries for the dates, adapted from a recipe on the Ambitious Kitchen website. Audrey suggests using fresh dates or dried apricots if you don't have fresh cherries on hand. What she likes best—and kids will, too—is that this is a very forgiving recipe; you can make it your own by playing with sugar amounts, fruit, flours, even the butter. You can use any kind of fresh or frozen cherry—either sour or sweet. Just vary the sweetness to your taste. This can also be a vegan dessert if you use vegan spread rather than butter.

Adult: Preheat the oven to 350 degrees, and line the baking pan with parchment paper. Set it aside.

Child with Adult: In a large bowl, use a fork to mix together the oat "flour," whole oats, brown sugar, cinnamon, baking soda, and salt.

Adult: Melt the butter in the saucepan.

Child: Add the butter and the vanilla extract to the dry ingredients. Mix with your fingers until the dough starts to clump together and a nice crumble forms, adding more butter or a tablespoon or so of water—if the dough doesn't hold together. This mixture will become both the bottom and top layers. Put 1½ cups or half the mixture into the prepared pan for the bottom crust, patting down the dough to make an even bottom layer, and put the rest of the dough, the top layer, mixed with the almonds (if using), into the fridge.

Adult with Child: To make the filling, pit the fresh cherries by putting one cherry inside the cherry pitter and carefully pressing until the pit slips through into a bowl or wide jar. Or, if you don't have a cherry pitter, hold a cherry in one hand and take a paper clip in the other; push the rounded end of the paperclip through the stem end of the cherry until you reach the pit, then hook the clip around the pit and pull it out. Do this over a bowl—it can be fun, but messy! »

EQUIPMENT

- Food processor or blender
- One 8-by-8-inch baking pan
- Parchment paper
- Large mixing bowl
- Fork
- Cherry pitter or paper clip
- Measuring cups
- Measuring spoons
- Medium saucepan
- Wooden spoon

Cherry Oatmeal Cookie Bars continued »

Adult with Child: Heat the cherries, maple syrup or sugar, cornstarch, almond extract, and salt in the saucepan, pressing down with a wooden spoon just a bit. Bring the mixture to a boil; then reduce the heat and cook for a few more minutes, until the mixture is thickened and coats the back of a spoon. Cool it a little, and then spread the cherry mixture evenly over the bottom crust.

Child: Take the remaining topping out of the fridge. Make sure the topping clumps a little. If it doesn't, chill it for a bit longer. Spread the top layer evenly over the cherry filling.

Adult: Bake for about 30 minutes, or until the topping gets a little golden. Cool it completely in the pan. Cut it into sixteen bars before serving.

PURIM

Falafel 145

Chopped Israeli Salad 146

Flynn's Orzo 147

Pita Bread 148

Hamantashen 151

Halvah 153

Lemon Yogurt Pound Cake 154

Purim Dinner

Challah*

Hummus*

Moroccan Apricot Chicken Tagine*

Couscous

Green Vegetables

Hamantashen*

Shalach Manot Plate

Hamantashen*

Aunt Lisl's Butter Cookies*

Peanut Butter–Stuffed Figs and Dates with Coconut*

Golda Meir's Chocolate Chip Cookies*

Chocolate Chip Kisses*

PURIM

Purim is a holiday on which we celebrate the Jewish people's deliverance from serious danger in the fifth century BCE. Haman, the minister of the Persian King Ahasuerus, wished to exterminate all the Jews of the Persian Empire, because he thought the Jew Mordecai had failed to show him proper respect by refusing to bow down to him. It was because Mordecai only bowed to God. Esther, Mordecai's cousin and foster daughter, became the second queen of King Ahasuerus but had to hide that she was Jewish. The two foiled wicked Haman's plot. On Adar 13, usually sometime in March, the day before present-day Purim, Haman decreed the Jews to be destroyed. Instead, the Jewish population overcame those who wanted to wipe them out and then celebrated their victory on Adar 14, the following day.

Mordecai and Esther proclaimed that the festival of Purim (meaning "lots") should be celebrated for all time, by two annual recountings of the story of the Megillah (the Book of Esther) in the synagogue (on the eve of Purim) followed by a *Seudat* Purim, or festival meal, in the late afternoon of Purim. Groggers, small noisemakers, are used to drown out Haman's name in the readings. To remind us that, despite living in the splendor of the King's palace, Esther never forgot her humble origins, we give charity to the poor, and we send gifts of small baked goods and candy, especially Hamantaschen (*shalach manot*), to friends and family. These are the four mitzvot of Purim.

Because Queen Esther had to mask her true identity, we wear costumes and masks at our Purim celebration. These days Vashti, the king's first wife, is a second heroine for refusing the king's unreasonable demands.

As Esther never forgot her humble origins, the humble chickpeas are traditionally eaten at Purim to remind children of her purity. You can eat them or use them as dried beans inside a decorated paper plate stapled together to make a *grogger*. One dish my children love to eat at Purim, or at any time, is hummus, which we use as a dip for cut-up vegetables or pieces of pita bread. And, of course, why not eat falafel, another happy and protein-filled dish made from chickpeas?

Finally, Purim, a festival of folly like Mardi Gras, places a greater emphasis on physical delights than does any other Jewish holiday. It is a holiday of letting go, drinking, and donning costumes and dancing in parades, parties, and carnivals, of preparing an elaborate meal at home, and of just having lots of fun. If you go to Israel, you see a real carnival atmosphere, people dancing in the streets in costumes and going from house to house delivering *shalach manot*.

Daniela and Merissa, as little girls, dressed up as Queen Esther, making crowns and sewing fancy dresses in which they would parade at synagogue. Since David dressed up for Purim (and all the time!), he delighted in dressing up as different Biblical characters.

All children love to sound their *groggers* whenever wicked Haman's name is mentioned during the reading of the Megillah. During the reading in our synagogue, even the clergy takes part, dressing up as popular characters of the moment.

FALAFEL

Makes about 24 patties

INGREDIENTS

- 2 cups dried chickpeas
- ½ cup fine bulgur
- 1 large onion, chopped
- 2 tablespoons finely chopped fresh parsley
- 1 large egg
- 1 teaspoon salt
- 1 teaspoon dried hot red pepper flakes
- 2 garlic cloves, peeled
- 1 teaspoon ground cumin
- Dash of ground coriander
- Vegetable oil, for deep-frying
- Pita bread
- Shaved lettuce
- Sour pickles or turnips
- Tahina
- Hot sauce

EQUIPMENT

- Measuring cups
- Measuring spoons
- Mixing bowl
- Blender or food processor
- Falafel maker (optional)
- Deep-fryer or heavy pot
- Slotted spoon
- Paper towels

Probably more than any other food eaten in Israel, falafel, the primary street food, has gained international status. It is eaten from street carts and tiny stores from Tel Aviv to Paris to Los Angeles to Cairo. Unlike falafel in other countries of the Middle East, falafel in Israel is made only with chickpeas, because many Middle Eastern Jews and Arabs have an enzymatic reaction to fava beans. Have a falafel party with your family.

Child with Adult: Place a large bowl of cold water on a table, and have the children pour the chickpeas into the bowl to soak them overnight. You can't leave the chickpeas too long, though, or, like a grain, they will sprout. At different times, show them how the legume grows!

Child with Adult: The next day, put the bulgur into a bowl, and cover it with water. Drain the chickpeas, and mix them with the onion. Add the parsley, egg, salt, pepper flakes, garlic, cumin, and coriander. Whirl this mixture in a blender or food processor. Drain the bulgur, mix it with the chickpeas, and continue to process until the mixture is smooth and able to form a small ball in your hand. Refrigerate it for at least 1 hour. Form the mixture into small balls, about the size of a walnut, or use a falafel maker to shape it, if you can find one.

Adult with Child: Flatten the patties slightly, and then deep-fry them in oil until they're golden brown on each side. Remove with a slotted spoon, and drain the falafel on paper towels. Stuff the falafel into pita bread with shaved lettuce, sour pickles or turnips, tahina, and hot sauce.

CHOPPED ISRAELI SALAD

Serves 4

INGREDIENTS

1 tomato

1 cucumber

2 scallions

2 tablespoons chopped fresh parsley

1 green pepper

1 lemon, at room temperature

6 tablespoons extra-virgin olive oil

1 clove garlic, mashed

Salt and freshly ground black pepper to taste

EQUIPMENT

Measuring spoons

Plastic knife

Cutting board

Knife

Fork

Small bowl

When I first visited Israel in 1970 salads were very often do-it-yourself affairs. Kibbutzniks had the custom of putting the raw ingredients on the table and letting everyone make individual salads.

For breakfast—often eaten at 4:00 a.m., so that the farm work could be done before the heat of day—workers ate at long tables. A large bowl was filled with whole green peppers, cucumbers, tomatoes, scallions, and sometimes kohlrabi. There were smaller bowls of olives, hard-boiled eggs, cheeses, and bread. Salad dressing was made with the lemons that grow locally. The food was cut up by diners into little pieces, and makeshift salads were prepared to the taste of the diners. Kibbutzim have changed and in most cases this custom is a thing of the past.

The following recipe is a great exercise for children in learning to use a knife. Give them a plastic knife for starters. You don't want to begin this until the children are four or five years old. And let them pick out their favorite vegetables for their own salads.

Adult with Child: Show the children how to hold a vegetable firmly with one hand and then, gently but firmly, cut a slice into the vegetable. Let them take turns until all the vegetables are diced (do not peel the tomato). Mix all the vegetables together in a bowl.

Child: Make sure the lemon is at room temperature; then cut it in half. Take a fork, and pierce the pulp of each side of the lemon. Then, using one hand like a strainer, with the other hand squeeze the lemon through your fingers, catching the seeds before they get mixed with the juice.

Child: Carefully sprinkle the lemon juice and then the oil over the vegetables. Add the garlic (unless you find garlic yucky), and season with salt and pepper as you like.

Note: You can also add black olives, carrots, kohlrabi, lettuce, or whatever you like. Or, as in an Israeli kibbutz, just place the freshly picked vegetables on the table and let people make their own salads, cutting up and seasoning as they go along.

FLYNN'S ORZO

Serves 4

INGREDIENTS

- 1 medium onion, diced
- 2 tablespoons extra-virgin olive oil
- 2 garlic cloves, minced
- 1 teaspoon dried oregano
- 15 ounces diced canned tomatoes
- 1 cup corn (frozen or fresh)
- 1 cup orzo
- ½ teaspoon salt
- ½ cup feta
- 2 tablespoons chopped fresh basil, for serving

EQUIPMENT

- Frying pan with a lid
- Sharp knife
- Measuring cup
- Measuring spoons
- Spoon, for stirring

Sometimes you need a recipe made of whatever is in the kitchen. When I asked Yotam Ottolenghi, who has two boys, if he would like to share a recipe with me for this cookbook, he responded immediately. "My youngest, Flynn, who is eight years old, invented a dish on school vacation when the family was in Northern Ireland, where we have a second home as my husband, Karl, is Irish," he wrote in an email. "We call it Flynn's Orzo and I am happy for you to formalize it into a recipe. Even though it was made with what we had in the cupboard, we all love it." It is surprisingly delicious, a good last-minute dish to serve to unexpected guests any time of the year. Feel free to vary the vegetables and cheese according to your children's taste! And I love Flynn's touch of not stirring the feta, so it stays in chunks when you serve it.

Adult with Child: Sauté the onion in the olive oil in a frying pan until it's soft and lightly browned; add the minced garlic for the last 3 minutes.

Child: Add the dried oregano and tomatoes, and cook for 5 to 10 minutes, stirring occasionally.

Adult with Child: Add the corn, orzo, 2 cups of water, and the salt. Bring the water to a boil; then lower the heat to simmer.

Child: Break up the feta into chunks, and push it into the orzo.

Adult with Child: Cover the pan with a lid, and cook for 10 minutes more, until most of the water is absorbed and the orzo is cooked. Leave the mixture to rest for 1 minute; then serve the dish sprinkled with chopped basil.

Makes 12 pitas

INGREDIENTS

1 package active dry yeast (or 1 scant tablespoon

1 tablespoon extra-virgin olive oil

2 tablespoons honey

1 tablespoon salt

About 4 to 5 cups unbleached all-purpose flour

EQUIPMENT

Two mixing bowls, one greased

Stand mixer

Towel

Dough cutter

Baking tiles or baking stone

Baking sheet

PITA BREAD

"And thou shalt take fine flour, and bake twelve cakes thereof: two tenths parts of an ephah shall be in one cake. And thou shalt set them in two rows, six in a row, upon the pure table before Adonai. And thou shalt put pure frankincense with each row, that it may be to the bread for a memorial-part, even an offering made by fire unto Adonai. Every sabbath day he shall set it in order before Adonai continually; it is from the children of Israel, an everlasting covenant."

—LEVITICUS 24:5–8

There is something magical and mysterious about pita bread. It puffs way up in the oven to become a pocket. And if you read the above quote, you might believe, as I do, that a form of pita must have been the original challah, using the local emmer wheat, the so-called mother of wheat originating in Israel or nearby. Most likely they were flat since emmer wheat has less gluten than our regular flour today that makes hearth breads like challah. Surely, the bread was neither sweet nor braided—those changes came after the Jews' expulsion from ancient Israel to Rome and then the rest of Europe. If the above citation from Leviticus is true, the "cake" must have been round, like pita bread. After all, how many forms of bread are there, anyway? Yemenite, Iraqi, all the ancient Jewish civilizations still use a form of round flattish bread for the Sabbath. Until recently, many people in Israel used two challahs, one like an Ashkenazic challah and one like a round pita. Today, there are puffy thick pitas and thinner pitas. Pita is so much fun to make, and can be done before the Sabbath as a throwback to the past. Just remember, the word "pita" comes from the ancient Greek word *pitter*, meaning "split." A baker at one of Mike Solomonov's restaurants in Philadelphia gave me a hint for encouraging the dough to split—roll the dough out, let the rounds rest a few minutes, and then, just before you put them into the hot oven, roll them out once more.

Child with Adult: Sprinkle the yeast into a large bowl, and pour 2 cups of warm water on top. Stir this until the yeast is dissolved; add the olive oil, honey, and salt, and mix well. Add enough flour so that the dough becomes difficult to stir. You can also throw everything into a stand mixer and use a dough hook to mix the dough.

Adult with Child: Turn the dough out onto a floured surface, and knead it for a few minutes; add more flour as necessary to make a firm, elastic dough. Place the dough into a greased bowl, and let it rise, covered, for about 1 hour or until doubled in bulk.

Child with Adult: Transfer the dough to a large floured surface and cut it into twelve equal sections. Using your hands, form each section into the shape and size of a Ping-Pong ball. Cover them with a towel, and set them aside for about 5 minutes.

Child with Adult: Flour the work surface lightly. Using a rolling pin, roll out each ball to a disk about 5 inches in diameter. The dough will be very elastic, so try adding a little more flour as necessary to keep the disks from sticking. Cover the circles, and let them rise for 15 minutes.

Adult: Line one rack of the oven with baking tiles or a baking stone and your baking sheet, and heat the oven to 500 degrees. (If you do not have either tiles or stone, merely heat your baking sheet.)

Adult with Child Watching: When the oven is really hot, roll out the dough one more time; then, quickly but gently, pick up the disks with your fingers and toss them onto the cookie sheet. Hopefully they will puff up in the oven! Bake them for 8 to 10 minutes. Remove the pitas with tongs or a spatula. Repeat with the remaining rounds.

HAMANTASHEN

Makes about 36 cookies

INGREDIENTS

DOUGH

- ⅔ cup (1⅓ sticks) unsalted butter or vegan spread, softened, or coconut oil
- ½ cup sugar
- 1 large egg
- 3 tablespoons milk or water
- ½ teaspoon vanilla extract
- 2½ to 3 cups sifted unbleached all-purpose flour
- ½ teaspoon salt

FILLINGS

- Apricot, strawberry, or prune preserves
- Peanut butter
- Chocolate chips
- Nutella
- Nuts
- Chopped apples

EQUIPMENT

- Measuring cups
- Measuring spoons
- Mixing bowl
- Wooden spoon
- Sifter
- Knife
- Rolling pin
- Baking sheets
- Spatula
- Cooling rack

Haman's hats are the most popular sweet made from flour at Purim. One legend tells us that the three corners of the cookie represent Abraham, Isaac, and Jacob, the founding fathers of Judaism. Although hamantashen traditionally include apricot, poppy seed, or prune filling, my children and grandchildren like them filled with peanut butter, jelly, Nutella, or even chocolate chips. Because of those slightly irregular chocolate chip hamantashen, Purim could become an everyday tradition as far as my children and grandchildren are concerned. Recently I was surprised to see these in the fall prominently displayed at a bakery in rural Maryland. When our children were little, we included them on the *shalach manot* plates we took to our neighbors, and now I mail some to my children and grandchildren . . . even though they often arrive in crumbles!

Child: Using a wooden spoon, cream the butter, vegan spread, or coconut oil with the sugar. Add the egg, and continue creaming until the mixture is smooth. Add the milk or water and vanilla. Mix the flour and salt, and mix this with the butter-sugar mixture until a ball of dough is formed. Divide the dough into two cylinders, each approximately 3 inches in diameter, and refrigerate them for a few hours or overnight. »

Hamantashen continued »

Adult: Preheat the oven to 350 degrees, and cover two baking sheets with parchment paper.

Child with Adult, Then Child Alone: Using one cylinder of dough at a time (keep the unused portion refrigerated until needed), cut ⅛-inch slices of dough. Roll the dough out on a floured board until ⅛ inch thick. Using a 2-inch cookie cutter, cut out circles and put 1 heaping teaspoon of filling in the center of each round. Draw the edges up at three points to form a triangle and pinch the sides together carefully, leaving a little opening in the center. Place the triangles on the baking sheets, and bake for about 20 minutes, or until golden brown. Cool on a rack.

Note: If your children are very young, prepare the dough yourself, and just let them make the cookies. You can also use a food processor to do this.

HALVAH

Makes about 20 squares

INGREDIENTS

- ¾ cup unbleached all-purpose flour
- ¾ cup tahini
- 1 cup sugar
- ½ teaspoon ground cinnamon
- ½ teaspoon ground cardamom
- ¾ cup vegetable oil
- 1 cup chopped pistachios or walnuts

EQUIPMENT

- Measuring cups
- Measuring spoon
- Large frying pan with cover
- Wooden spoon
- Spatula
- 8-x-8-inch square pan

Persian Jews from present-day Iran are especially proud of Queen Esther's role in the holiday of Purim. A favorite dish of all children in Iran is halvah—a candy with ancient roots, which Persian Jews eat after they break the Fast of Esther, observed on Adar 13. At nursery school, Merissa learned this recipe for halvah from an Iranian teacher. In between bites, the children played with Esther and Ahasuerus marionettes they had made with the help of their teacher. This recipe was originally not sesame based, but I have adapted it since to include tahini. Its texture is more spoonable than cuttable, quite different from the commercial halvah to which we are accustomed.

Adult with Child: In a frying pan, brown the flour over low heat for about 20 minutes, watching constantly and stirring occasionally with a wooden spoon. Remove the pan from the heat.

Child: To the flour, add the tahini, sugar, cinnamon, cardamom, and all but a tablespoon of the oil. With the pan still off the heat, stir for about 5 minutes, keeping the mixture a light-brown color.

Adult with Child: Add 1 cup of water and reheat, whisking for 2 to 3 minutes, until the halvah thickens. Then remove from the heat and cover the pan for a few minutes. Fold in the pistachios or walnuts.

Child: Using the remaining tablespoon of vegetable oil, grease an 8-inch square pan. Then scoop the mixture into the pan, spreading out well.

Child: Let the mixture cool completely in the refrigerator and then cut it into small squares.

LEMON YOGURT POUND CAKE

Makes 1 cake, serving about 12

INGREDIENTS

- Vegetable spray
- 2¼ cups unbleached all-purpose flour
- 1½ cups granulated sugar
- ½ teaspoon salt
- ½ teaspoon baking soda
- Grated zest of 1 lemon
- 1 teaspoon vanilla extract
- 1 cup (2 sticks) unsalted butter, vegan spread, or coconut oil
- 1 cup lemon yogurt
- 3 large eggs

GLAZE

- 1 cup confectioners' sugar
- 2 tablespoons lemon juice

EQUIPMENT

- Measuring cups
- Measuring spoons
- 10-inch Bundt or tube pan
- Large mixing bowl
- Stand mixer

I always think of this as "a giving cake," because my late cousin Dorothy often gave this to me on my birthday, and gave it as a present to other people as well, many times throughout the year. So why not present this to your neighbors at Purim on your *shalach manot* plates instead of cookies? And involve your children by inviting them to choose the kind of yogurt they want to use in the cake.

Adult: Preheat the oven to 325 degrees.

Child: Grease a 10-inch Bundt or tube pan with vegetable spray.

Adult with Child: Measure the flour, granulated sugar, salt, and baking soda into a mixing bowl. In the bowl of a stand mixer, mix 1 teaspoon of the lemon zest; the vanilla; butter, vegan spread, or coconut oil; yogurt; and eggs. Fold in the flour ingredients, and pour the batter into the greased pan. Bake for 60 to 70 minutes, or until the cake springs back when touched. Cool it in the pan for 15 minutes. Remove it, and let it cool completely.

Child: Combine the confectioners' sugar, the lemon juice, and the remaining lemon zest, and drizzle the mixture over the cake. Serve it as is.

PASSOVER

Nut-Free Haroset 162
A Seder Salad 163
Vegetable Kugelettes 165
Matzo Pizza 166
Passover-Style Farfel and Cheese 168
Matzo Brei 169
Almond Caramel Chocolate Matzo Brittle 170
Passover Chocolate Almond Cake 173
Chocolate Chip Kisses 175

Child-Centered Seder Menu

Chicken Soup with Matzo Balls*

Roast Turkey

Vegetable Kugelettes*

A Seder Salad*

Fresh Strawberries

Passover Chocolate Almond Cake*

Passover Lunch

Matzo Pizza*

Cut-Up Veggies

Almond Caramel Chocolate Matzo Brittle*

PASSOVER

> *And they shall eat the flesh in that night, roast with fire, and unleavened bread; with bitter herbs they shall eat it. Eat not of it raw, nor sodden at all with water, but roast with fire; its head with its legs and with the innards thereof.*
>
> EXODUS 12:8–9

Passover, easily the most celebrated Jewish holiday in America today, has followed the Biblical directives to eat a meal of roast lamb, bitter herbs, and matzo (unleavened bread) for thousands of years. Starting as an ancient spring festival, it eventually became the ritual surrounding the defining moment of Judaism, when the Israelites left Egypt for the promised land: when Jews became Jews. As such, it has been celebrated all over the world with small changes throughout history. In my home, the festive Seder (meaning "order") meal on the first night of Passover, which tells the story of the flight from slavery to freedom, is the most eagerly awaited family event of the year. Whenever I am preparing for it, I get very emotional, seeing that my family, in our way, is putting together one of the oldest theatrically produced meals known to mankind. At the Seder the participants are reminded of the rich heritage of thousands of years of both suffering and deliverance through those millennia, aided by the reading of the Haggadah and by the symbolic foods eaten throughout the meal. Although many hold two Seders, I do not. Often we are invited to another Seder or have a simple dinner at home where we continue discussions.

Pesach means "passing by" or "passing over," and the holiday was called Passover because Adonai passed over the Jewish houses when, for the tenth and last plague, He slew the firstborn of Egypt. Matzo, unleavened and quickly baked, recalls that the Jews fleeing Egypt had no time to leaven their bread and to bake it properly. Thus, we eat no leavened products throughout the eight days of Passover.

Three matzot are placed on the Seder table. One half of one matzo is set aside and served later to mark the ceremonial end of the Seder. It is called the *afikomen,* based on a Greek word for "dessert." Traditionally, the *afikomen* is hidden at the beginning of the Seder, and the children search for it at the end—a wonderful way of sustaining their interest throughout the long meal! In fact, the Seder is designed to engage children from start to finish, through tastes, songs, questions, and even games.

Before the Seder, the children help me arrange the symbolic foods on the Seder plate:

Salt water: This represents the bitter tears shed during the years of slavery and the water needed in the spring to make things grow.

Maror: Grated horseradish, bitter herbs, or romaine lettuce are a reminder of the bitterness of slavery.

Zeroa: A roasted shank bone symbolizes the ancient sacrificial lamb of the Passover service and the rebirth of nature in the spring.

Haroset: A mixture of apples, nuts, cinnamon, and wine represents the mortar used by Jewish slaves to build pyramids for the Pharaohs. Since each diasporic culture has its own recipe, to me this tells about the wandering nature of the Jewish people and how all these recipes have come to Israel.

Karpas: Parsley, or some other available green, recalls the green of the spring and the renewal of faith and hope.

Betzah: A hard-boiled egg, boiled and then darkened with a lit match in its shell, represents life and the continuity of existence, as well as recalling the special festival offering in the days of the Temple of Jerusalem.

If you don't have special Seder plates and cups collected through generations as I do, Seder plates and cups are easy for the children to make. Don't forget to have a cup for the prophet Elijah or one for Miriam, who helped her brother Moses shepherd the children to freedom. Wine cups made of plastic can be decorated with permanent marking pens. Colorful paper plates with cupcake holders glued on are very successful as Seder plates. When our children were little, we had an adult table and a children's table, so I needed two Seder plates. During the service itself, the children always sat with us.

Children can make their own Haggadahs at school or at home and then have them on the table. We saved our children's for years, and I put them out at the Seder. We also make getting ready for Passover a family spring-cleaning affair. The children help clean their rooms, and go through their closets, and it is a good time to donate unneeded items.

The kitchen is left for last, with all the *chametz,* or leavened products, brought to the garage. (Some families symbolically sell their *chametz* to neighbors and buy it back at the end of Passover. From Purim to Passover, we try to use up all our flour, rice, and cereals, so there is not much to get rid of.) Traditional families have separate sets of dishes for the eight days of Passover. The day before the holiday, some take a feather, or the lulav saved from Sukkot, and symbolically look for *chametz* around the house. When the children were little, I planted some pieces of bread for them to find before I threw the bread out.

The day of the Seder is one of the busiest of the year for me, getting ready for about forty guests each time. When my children were young, I kept them occupied with coloring and decorating name tags, setting the table, and helping to make the haroset, one of the last dishes to be prepared for the Seder.

We have always tried to make our Seder as participatory as possible: dipping a finger in wine, making everyone taste the bitter herbs and parsley, and singing the songs. But what really makes our Seder different from most is that the children always perform a Passover play. They put together a skit of the exodus of the Jews from Egypt. The characters are always the same—God, baby Moses and grown-up Moses, Aaron, Pharoah, sheep, Miriam—and it is always hysterical and different depending on the players, aged four years old to ninety-four!

NUT-FREE HAROSET

Makes about 2 cups

INGREDIENTS

2 cups dates, pitted

1 cup warm water

½ teaspoon ground ginger

2 tablespoons sweet red wine or grape juice

EQUIPMENT

Small saucepan

Measuring cup

Measuring spoons

Old-fashioned chopper or food processor

This haroset comes from the Greek island of Rhodes, and it usually includes a cup of walnuts. What I like about this version is that you can make it kid-friendly, without the nuts in the original recipe. (If you'd like nuts, add 1 cup walnuts when you process the dates.) Serve this as the last food of the Passover Seder, on top of matzo; crunchy romaine lettuce can be the bitter herb, instead of the bitter horseradish root used by Ashkenazic Jews.

Child: Put the dates into a small saucepan, and pour the water over them. Soak them for about 20 minutes, and then simmer until they're slightly soft, 5 to 10 minutes.

Child with Adult: Put the dates through a Mouli grinder if you have one, or pulse in a food processor. Add the ginger and wine or grape juice to the grinder or food processor, and slowly process again.

A SEDER SALAD

INGREDIENTS

Carrots
Black olives
Green peppers
Parboiled asparagus
Romaine lettuce leaves
Raisins
Radishes
Vinaigrette dressing

EQUIPMENT

Vegetable peeler
Paring knife

I find the Seder preparation such a strenuous task that, the more I can allow my children and rambunctious grandchildren to create, the better it is for me. They design this dish for each person and have fun doing it. Depending on the age of your children, you can have the ingredients cut up ahead of time and just let them do the assembling.

Adult with Child: Peel the carrots, and slice them into rounds and cut the olives in half. Cut the green peppers and asparagus into strips as long as you want for your salad.

Child: Place a romaine leaf on each salad plate, as a cradle or little ark. Using the salad vegetables, decorate it as you would imagine a baby Moses in his cradle, with his face, arms, and so on.

Child with Adult: If you wish, add radish flowers for decoration. These are made by carefully cutting off the top of a radish and then slicing down the sides, about one-third of the way down, in four or five places.

Child: Remember that adults like dressing, which you can drizzle on top of the salad. They also tend to like asparagus better than you do.

VEGETABLE KUGELETTES

Makes 24

INGREDIENTS

- 2 apples
- 1 large sweet potato
- 4 carrots
- 1 cup matzo meal
- ½ cup (1 stick) unsalted dairy or vegan butter, melted, or vegetable oil
- 1 teaspoon salt
- 1 teaspoon baking soda*
- 1 teaspoon ground cinnamon
- 1 teaspoon ground nutmeg
- ½ cup light- or dark-brown sugar

EQUIPMENT

- Measuring cups
- Measuring spoon
- Vegetable peeler
- Grater or food processor
- Mixing bowl
- Wooden spoon
- Twenty-four paper muffin cups
- Muffin tins for 24 cupcakes
- Rubber scraper

* Baking soda is kosher for Passover.

A kugel, usually a bread pudding cooked with the Sabbath cholent, was the kind of slightly sweet Eastern European dish we think of as dessert. Sugary desserts were actually a very late invention. I have turned this kugel, a very old and beloved recipe from the Feinberg family of Cincinnati, into little muffins or kugelettes.

Adult: Preheat the oven to 325 degrees.

Child: Place the paper muffin cups in the muffin tins.

Child Alone, or with Adult: Peel, core, and grate the apples, and peel and grate the sweet potato and carrots, and measure so that each makes 1 cup, putting them into a bowl as you go. Mix in the matzo meal, your choice of melted fat, the salt, baking soda, cinnamon, nutmeg, and brown sugar. Spoon the batter into the cups, making them two-thirds full. Bake, covered, for 20 minutes, then raise the oven to 350 degrees, remove the cover, and bake for an additional 15 minutes or until a toothpick comes out clean.

MATZO PIZZA

Serves 1

INGREDIENTS

1 matzo

½ cup tomato sauce

½ cup grated Parmesan or cheddar cheese (kosher for Passover)

EQUIPMENT

Baking sheet

Measuring cups

Spoon

Who doesn't love pizza? This is an easy substitute for lunch or dinner during Passover. Use your imagination here and add the vegetable or herb of your choice.

Adult: Preheat the oven to 400 degrees.

Child: Place the matzo on the baking sheet. Spread the tomato sauce on top, covering as much as you can. Sprinkle the cheese over the sauce.

Adult with Child: Bake the matzo pizza for about 5 minutes, or until the top is melted and bubbly. Remove from the oven to a plate, and enjoy eating it with a knife and fork or just your hands.

PASSOVER-STYLE FARFEL AND CHEESE

Serves 8

INGREDIENTS

- 3 large eggs
- 3 cups matzo farfel or matzo broken up into ½-inch pieces
- Vegetable spray
- ½ pound cheddar cheese
- 1½ cups sour cream
- 6 tablespoons (¾ stick) unsalted butter
- 2 cups milk
- 1 teaspoon salt
- ¼ teaspoon freshly ground black pepper

EQUIPMENT

- Measuring cups
- Measuring spoons
- Old-fashioned egg beater or wire whisk
- Mixing bowl
- Knife
- Spoon
- 2-quart baking dish with cover

It seems to me that every article about Passover food stresses food for the Seder itself. What about those in-between meals, when you cannot let the children have their usual macaroni and cheese, pizza, or hamburgers on buns? One of Merissa's nursery teachers taught us this recipe and I used it during the week of Passover with vegetables on the side.

Adult with Child: This is a great opportunity to talk about the old days, when you were young and used an egg beater! Break two of the eggs, and beat them well with the egg beater or whisk.

Child: Pour the beaten eggs over the farfel or matzo pieces and mix well. Pour this into the baking dish, which you've greased with vegetable spray.

Adult: Preheat the oven to 350 degrees.

Child: Being careful with the knife, dice the cheddar cheese into small bits. Add the cheese to the farfel or matzo pieces. Using a spoon, add the sour cream in dollops, and dot the mixture with butter. Mix together the milk, remaining egg, salt, and pepper, and pour this over the casserole. (A child can be very creative in this preparation, because basically it doesn't matter in the final product.)

Child with Adult: Cover the baking dish, and bake it for 30 minutes. Uncover, and let the top brown for 10 to 15 minutes more. Spoon it out onto plates.

MATZO BREI

Serves 4 to 6

INGREDIENTS

3 matzos

2 large eggs

Salt, to taste

1 tablespoon honey, plus (optional) more for serving

½ teaspoon ground cinnamon

2 tablespoons (¼ stick) unsalted butter or vegan spread for frying

Cinnamon sugar for serving

EQUIPMENT

Measuring spoons

Mixing bowl

Paper towels

Fork or wire whisk

Spoon

Frying pan

Metal spatula

What would Passover be without matzo brei for breakfast? Our family tradition, from my mother-in-law, was to soak a matzo carefully in water and then, ever so carefully, try to remove it in one piece before drenching it in eggs. The next generation found that too hard, so we worked together on this variation of a classic theme. And still, everyone has an opinion on how to make matzo brei and what condiments to use on top. Good luck!

Child: Break up the matzos and soak them in lukewarm water for a few minutes. Drain them on paper towels, and squeeze them dry. Beat the eggs. Mix them well with the salt, honey, cinnamon, and the matzo.

Adult: Heat the butter or vegan spread in the frying pan. Fry 2 tablespoons of batter at a time, patting the center down a bit. Turn the pieces over, and fry them until golden on both sides. Eat them as they are, or drizzled with additional honey or sprinkled with cinnamon sugar.

Makes 6 cups

INGREDIENTS

4 matzos

1 cup unsalted butter or vegan spread, cut into 1-tablespoon pieces

1 cup firmly packed dark-brown sugar

1 cup good-quality bittersweet chocolate, broken into pieces or chips or chunks

2 tablespoons water

1 cup coarsely chopped toasted almonds

½ teaspoon flaky salt

EQUIPMENT

Baking sheet (see procedure for dimensions)

Parchment paper

Medium saucepan

Wooden spoon, for stirring

Heatproof spatula

Microwavable cup

ALMOND CARAMEL CHOCOLATE MATZO BRITTLE

Although I, like so many others, drizzled chocolate over matzo each year for my children at Passover, I somehow missed the creation of "Caramel Matzo Crunch"—also called "buttercrunch," "matzo crack," or "brittle" and found in many incarnations in various cookbooks, blogs, and websites. As with so many Internet recipes today, sometimes the provenance is acknowledged, but mostly not.

Being the food detective that I am, I thought I'd set the record straight. The instant classic comes from Marcy Goldman, author of *A Treasury of Jewish Holiday Baking*, originally published in 1998. In the book she includes a recipe that she calls "My Trademark, Most Requested, Absolutely Magnificent Caramel Matzoh Crunch."

Occasionally, guests have brought this brittle to my Passover Seder; it never strayed too far from the original.

Today, most people still make Marcy's dessert with chocolate and maybe almonds. I've also made it with peanut butter instead of chocolate, but my grandchildren like chocolate with crunchy almonds. I add flaky salt to counter the sweetness. You can try it with other nut butters, like almond or cashew, or, to be even more decadent, tahini with a sprinkle of halvah. Just beware: no matter how you make this sweet, it is totally addictive. And remember, brittle is best—and at its snappiest—when chilled.

Adult: Heat the oven to 375 degrees, and line a rimmed 11-by-17- or 12-by-18-inch baking sheet with parchment paper, covering the pan and extending over the sides.

Adult with Child: Lay two matzo squares in the pan, positioning the convex side up to best retain the chocolate. Then, like a puzzle, fit the remaining matzos onto the baking sheet, carefully breaking pieces to fill the entire baking pan in one layer. (Don't worry if they are not perfect; the brittle will be cut up later.)

Adult: In a medium saucepan, melt the butter or vegan spread and brown sugar over medium heat, stirring constantly, until the mixture comes to a boil, about 5 minutes. Boil just until it's very bubbly, another 2 to 3 minutes, and remove the saucepan from the heat.

Child with Adult: Carefully let the child pour the caramel over the matzo, covering it completely. Working quickly, spread the caramel with a heatproof spatula, then spoon it on top, trying not to let it spill between the matzos. (Once the residual caramel cools in the pot, dip your fingers in to taste it—a necessary first step to cleaning up!)

Adult: Put the baking sheet into the oven, and reduce the temperature to 325 degrees. Bake for 10 to 12 minutes, checking to make sure the edges and top are not burning.

Child with Adult: While the brittle is baking, heat the chocolate with the water in a cup in a microwave until it's melted and easily pourable, about 20 seconds on high.

Adult with Child: Remove the matzo from the oven, and let the child drizzle the warm chocolate on top; then sprinkle it with the almonds, and then with the salt. Let it cool, break it into pieces, and transfer them to a container lined with parchment paper. Refrigerate for at least 30 minutes, or freeze for 15, until the chocolate firms up. Let it thaw for about 10 minutes before serving, and watch it be gobbled up. (The second step of cleaning up is to lick the chocolate left in the cup.)

Note: You can also do a very simple version of this recipe. Heat up the chocolate and water in a microwave; using tongs, just dip the matzos into the melted chocolate; put it on wax paper to cool. Refrigerate it until you're ready to serve it.

לחם

PASSOVER CHOCOLATE ALMOND CAKE

Makes one 9-inch cake

INGREDIENTS

2 scant cups chopped dark chocolate (11 ounces; at least 60 percent cacao)

8 tablespoons (1 stick) unsalted butter or vegan spread, softened, or coconut oil

¾ cup sugar

Big pinch of salt

4 large eggs, lightly beaten

½ cup almond flour

EQUIPMENT

Measuring cups

9-inch round or square cake pan

Parchment paper

Microwavable bowl

Stand mixer, or hand mixer and big bowl

Flexible spatula

Offset spatula

Toothpick

Wire cooling rack

This delicious gluten-free cake that chef Mike Solomonov of Zahav Restaurant in Philadelphia makes will become a favorite all year long with the whole family. What I like best about it is that it reminds me of French cakes that my friends' mothers in France used to make for birthdays, which the chef Jean-Georges Vongerichten gave celebrity status when he slightly undercooked it and renamed the dessert "molten chocolate cake." My grandchildren thought the cake needed a bit less sugar, so we made that change. »

Passover Chocolate Almond Cake continued »

Adult: Preheat the oven to 375 degrees, with the rack in the middle. Line the bottom of a 9-inch round or square cake pan with parchment paper. Melt the chocolate in the microwave, and let it cool.

Child with Adult: Mix the butter, vegan spread, or coconut oil, sugar, and salt in the bowl of a stand mixer fitted with the paddle attachment (or use a hand mixer and a big bowl), and beat on medium-high speed until the mixture is pale and fluffy, about 2 minutes. Then add the melted chocolate, and mix just until it's combined. Scrape down the sides of the bowl with a flexible spatula and mix for another few seconds. With the mixer on low speed, add the eggs one at a time, beating until each one is incorporated before adding the next. Scrape down the sides of the bowl again; then add the almond flour, and mix on low until it's just incorporated, about 10 seconds.

Adult: Pour the batter into the prepared cake pan.

Child: Smooth the top with an offset spatula.

Adult with Child: Put the pan into the oven, and bake until a toothpick inserted in the center of the cake comes out clean, about 25 minutes. Let it cool in the pan for 10 minutes before turning it out onto a wire rack to cool completely.

CHOCOLATE CHIP KISSES

Makes about 36

INGREDIENTS

⅓ cup walnuts
⅓ cup pecans
3 large eggs
1 cup sugar
½ teaspoon vanilla extract (optional)
⅓ cup chocolate chips

EQUIPMENT

Measuring cups
Measuring spoon
Large mixing bowl
2 smaller mixing bowls
Electric mixer or wire whisk
Large spoon
Parchment paper
Baking sheets
Pancake turner

Young children love to make these, and it's a good lesson in separating egg yolks and whites.

Adult: Preheat the oven to 300 degrees.

Child: Break up the nuts into pieces no bigger than the chocolate chips, or smaller. Separate the eggs—one at a time, in case they break. Here's the Greek Jewish way: Make a tiny hole in one end of the egg. Holding the shell in the middle, let the white run out into a bowl. Save the yolks for another use. Here's the way I do it: crack the egg over a bowl, letting the white fall out, then carefully pour the yolk from one shell half to the other to remove the rest of the white. If I'm cracking more than one egg, I always do this in separate bowls, in case a yolk breaks or a shell falls into the whites.

Adult with Child: Beat the egg whites until they form peaks. Gradually beat in the sugar and vanilla until the whites are stiff.

Child: Gently stir the nuts and chocolate chips into the egg whites with a spoon. Drop the batter on parchment paper on a baking sheet in teardrops. Bake for 20 to 30 minutes, until the kisses are hard but still white.

Note: For children who don't like or can't eat nuts, simply substitute more chocolate chips.

SHAVUOT

Homemade Butter . . . 182
Homemade Curd Cheese . . . 183
Bagels . . . 186
Apple and Cream Cheese Spread . . . 188
Persian Cucumber-Yogurt Salad . . . 189
Cheese Blintzes . . . 190
Saffron's Easy French Toast . . . 191
Aunt Lorraine's Noodle Kugel . . . 192
Date Tahini Banana Milkshake . . . 194
Watermelon, Corn, Cucumber, and Feta Salad . . . 196
Apricot Fruit Leathers . . . 198

Shavuot Brunch

Bagels*

Homemade Butter*

Apple and Cream Cheese Spread*

Cheese Blintzes* or Saffron's Easy French Toast*

Fresh Strawberries and Oranges

Zucchini Bread*

Shavuot Lunch

Crustless Quiche with Cherry Tomatoes, Basil, and Cheese*

Green Salad

Aunt Lorraine's Noodle Kugel*

Date Tahini Banana Milkshake*

Lemon Yogurt Pound Cake*

SHAVUOT

A mountain of Adonai is the mountain of Bashan;
A mountain of peaks is the mountain of Bashan,
Why look ye askance, ye mountains of peaks,
At the mountain which Adonai hath desired for His abode?
Yea, Adonai will dwell therein forever.

—PSALM 68:16-17

Shavuot, or the festival of weeks, coming seven weeks after Passover when barley was planted, is the holiday not only marking the wheat harvest but it is also the day when Moses received the Torah, which includes the Ten Commandments, on Mount Sinai. And, as the above psalm points out, Mount Sinai, the place where Adonai revealed the Ten Commandments, has many different names, including Mountain of Adonai, Mountain of Bashan, and Mountain of Peaks. Another name, Gavunim, means "many peaked," with the same root as *gevinah,* the word for cheese.

All this means that Mount Sinai could also be called "Cheese Mountain," so eating cheese during this holiday reminds us of the giving of the Law. Shavuot started as a nature holiday celebrating the time when farmers brought the first fruits of their barley harvest to the Temple in Jerusalem.

Makes about ¼ cup or ½ stick per child

INGREDIENTS

½ cup heavy cream or whole milk per child

EQUIPMENT

Jar with a secure cap

HOMEMADE BUTTER

Shavuot is the perfect time to show children how to make their own butter because it falls at the time of year when cream and milk are traditionally the richest the world over, due to the abundance of green grass and other herbs eaten by goats, sheep, and cows that then produce more milk. Churning and cheesemaking are common features of spring harvest festivals most everywhere.

Child: Pour the cream or milk into the jar. Tighten the cap and shake the jar until the cream separates into butter and whey or liquid. This can take anywhere from a few minutes to 20 minutes, depending on the vigor of the shaking. Pour off the whey and use it as milk in baking.

HOMEMADE CURD CHEESE

Makes one 1-pound or two 8-ounce rounds

INGREDIENTS

½ gallon whole milk

2 tablespoons plain full-fat yogurt

3 ounces apple cider or white wine vinegar

2 teaspoons salt

About ½ cup diced fresh herbs such as parsley, tarragon, or dill

EQUIPMENT

Big pot

Pot holder

Spoon

Slotted spoon

Small bowl

Cheesecloth or porous dish towel

Homemade curd cheese is the most basic of any cheese. When I was in Israel recently, I visited the Iza Pziza Dairy Visitor Center with a group I was leading for Academic Travel Abroad. Together, we learned the magic of cheese making. We all had such fun making cheese that I was eager to take the recipe and technique home to show my grandchildren. So, when I returned to the States, we made it with some of my grandchildren's friends, and it was as magical for them as it was for the adults in Israel. »

Homemade Curd Cheese continued »

Child with Adult: Pour the milk into a large pot, and bring it almost to a boil, then turn off the heat. Add the yogurt and the vinegar; stir slowly but constantly with a spoon until the milk turns into curds. Allow the curds to sink and pour as much whey (cheese water) as possible into a sieve over a bowl. Reserve the whey and use it instead of milk in baking and for cereal. (The farm feeds the whey back to the goats.)

Adult with Child: Using a slotted spoon, transfer the curds to a bowl, season them with salt, and mix in the herbs; then add a bit of whey, and leave it for an hour in a covered container. Wrap up the cheese in a 12-by-12-inch piece of cheesecloth or a slightly porous dish towel, and mold it with your hands into a round, if you like. It is delicious with good bread, and even more delicious because the children made it themselves.

Makes 12 bagels

INGREDIENTS

1 tablespoon unsalted butter or vegan spread

1 cup cow's or vegan milk, scalded

1 scant tablespoon (1 package) active dry yeast

Pinch of sugar

2½ to 3 cups unbleached all-purpose flour, plus more for dusting

2 teaspoons salt

3 quarts water

1 tablespoon honey

Sesame, poppy, or nigella seeds

EQUIPMENT

Measuring spoons

Measuring cups

Small glass bowl

Large mixing bowl

Spoon

Greased mixing bowl

Clean dish towel

Large pot with lid

Slotted spoon

Greased baking sheet

BAGELS

There is no recipe more traditionally Jewish or more fun for children to make than bagels. In Judaism, bagels have a role in many life-cycle events. Because they're round, they symbolize the endless circle of life. They are traditionally served at circumcisions, naming ceremonies, and to break the fast of Yom Kippur, to name a few occasions.

This recipe comes from the late Mark Talisman, who baked throughout his whole life. When his daughter, Jessica, was a toddler, he tried to figure out a productive, creative, and tactile activity for her from 5:00 a.m., when she woke up, until 7:00, when the rest of the family awakened. Bagel making was the answer. Dough is more fun than clay; she could eat the bagels; and, when her younger brother, Rafi, came along, he could teethe on the lopsided figure eights she and her father made for him.

When you are making these with children, please don't be a perfectionist. Any roundish shape will do.

Adult with Child: Put the butter or vegan spread and the cow's or vegan milk in a glass bowl and microwave for about 30 seconds or until the butter is melted. Remove from the microwave. Mix the yeast with a pinch of sugar in ½ cup of warm water, and make sure it bubbles. Then add the milk mixture to the large bowl. Gradually blend in the flour and the salt, until a soft, sticky dough is formed. Knead it well, and place it in a greased bowl. Cover this with a clean towel, and let the dough rise in a warm place about 1 hour, until it has grown to almost double its size.

Child: Knead the dough again on a floured surface. Break off a piece about the size of a plum, and roll it into a 5½-inch-long snakelike shape, tapering the dough at the ends. Twist it into a circle, and press the ends together. Place it on a floured surface. Continue until all the dough is used. Let the bagels stand, uncovered, until the dough begins to rise (about 10 minutes).

Adult: Preheat the oven to 450 degrees. Boil about 3 quarts of water with the honey in a large pot.

Adult First, Then Child: Drop the bagels one by one into the boiling honey water, and boil a few at a time. Cover the pot, and wait until the water boils again. With a slotted spoon, turn the bagels over, cover the pot again, and wait until the water boils once more (1 to 2 minutes). Remove the bagels to a greased baking sheet. Repeat the boiling process with the remaining bagels.

Child: Sprinkle the bagels with sesame or poppy or nigella seeds, and bake them for 15 to 20 minutes, or until they're golden, rotating the pan about halfway through. These bagels freeze well.

Note: To shorten the waiting time for impatient children, do the first step yourself. Let the dough rise, and refrigerate it until you are ready to use it.

APPLE AND CREAM CHEESE SPREAD

Makes ½ cup

INGREDIENTS

1 small apple

½ teaspoon ground cinnamon

1 teaspoon sugar

4 ounces cream cheese

EQUIPMENT

Measuring spoons

Vegetable peeler

Apple corer

Food processor

Child: Carefully peel the apple and remove the core.

Adult with Child: Using the steel blade of the food processor, whirl together the apple and all the remaining ingredients. Spread on a bagel.

PERSIAN CUCUMBER-YOGURT SALAD

Serves 4 to 6

INGREDIENTS

- 2 small cucumbers
- 1 apple
- 2 hard-boiled eggs
- 1 cup yogurt
- ¼ cup white or dark raisins or pomegranate arils
- ¼ cup chopped walnuts or pistachio nuts
- Salt, to taste
- 3 tablespoons chopped fresh dill
- 2 tablespoons chopped mint

EQUIPMENT

- Measuring cups
- Measuring spoon
- Vegetable peeler
- Knife
- Glass or ceramic bowl
- Wooden spoon

Yogurt is probably the oldest milk dish in the world. The origin tale goes something like this. Once upon a time, a man who was going to ride a camel across the desert put some goat or sheep milk into his pouch. After he finished his journey and tasted the milk, it had changed into yogurt.

Child: Peel the cucumbers, apple, and eggs. Dice them, and put them into a glass or ceramic bowl. Stir in the yogurt, 1 cup of water, 3 ice cubes, the raisins or pomegranate arils, the walnuts or pistachios, and salt to taste. Cover the bowl, and let the salad sit in the refrigerator for a few hours. Just before serving, sprinkle on the fresh dill and mint, then mix together all the ingredients very well.

CHEESE BLINTZES

Makes about 2 dozen

INGREDIENTS

FILLING

- 1 pound cottage or ricotta cheese
- ¼ cup cream cheese
- 1 large egg
- 2 tablespoons matzo meal or all-purpose flour
- ¼ cup sugar

BLINTZES

- 2 cups unbleached all-purpose flour
- 1 cup milk
- 5 large eggs
- 2 tablespoons potato starch
- Butter, for frying
- Sour cream, for serving
- Blueberries, for serving

EQUIPMENT

- Measuring cups
- Measuring spoons
- Mixing bowls
- Blender
- Wax paper
- 6-inch nonstick skillet or crêpe pan

In the last edition of this book, I included cheese blintzes made out of white bread. No more. Even the youngest cook wants to make the real deal, because they've seen others their age preparing complicated dishes online. These blintzes, based on my mother's friend Dottie Licht's recipe, are basically rolled crêpes with a cottage cheese filling. Since dairy is essential at Shavuot, once you have figured out how to roll the crêpes carefully, they're a breeze, and great fun for children to make. My grandson, Aviv, was so proud of himself when he made a crêpe—I mean a blintz—the first time.

Child: To make the filling, mix together the cottage or ricotta cheese, cream cheese, egg, matzo meal or flour, and sugar in a bowl. Chill the mixture in the refrigerator for at least 1 hour.

Child with Adult: To make the blintzes, put the flour, 1½ cups water, the milk, the five large eggs, and the potato starch into the bowl of a blender, in two batches. Blend each batch for 30 seconds to 1 minute, until combined. Pour both into a bowl, and let the batter rest for 30 minutes.

Adult with Child: Grease a 6-inch nonstick skillet or crêpe pan with butter, and set it over medium heat. Pour a small ladle of the batter, about 2 tablespoons, into the pan. Tilt the pan slowly so the batter covers the bottom, then pour off any excess. Cook until the pancake blisters, but do not turn it. Flip the pancake onto wax paper, cooked side up. Repeat to cook all the batter, stacking the crêpes.

Child with Adult: Spread 1 heaping tablespoon of cheese filling along one end of the pancake. Turn the opposite side in, and roll it up like an envelope. Repeat to fill all the blintzes. Refrigerate them until you're ready to serve.

Child with Adult: Just before serving, fry the blintzes in more butter or oil until they're golden on both sides, and warm in the center, then serve them with sour cream and blueberries.

SAFFRON'S EASY FRENCH TOAST

Serves 4 to 6

INGREDIENTS

5 large eggs
1 cup milk
1 cup heavy cream
1 tablespoon sugar
1¼ teaspoon salt
1¼ teaspoon vanilla
5 or 6 slices of thickly sliced challah
1 tablespoon butter
Maple syrup, for serving

EQUIPMENT

Medium mixing bowl
Plate
Whisk
Nonstick large frying pan
Spatula

Los Angeles Chef Ori Menashe of Bavel, Bestia, and Saffy made up this easy kid-friendly French toast recipe with his daughter, Saffron. It takes minutes to make, is fun to prepare, and is delicious to eat. The brilliance of the recipe is using a mixing bowl in which you can soak all the slices of bread at once, making it really fun and fast. Then lift them out, drain them, and fry them briefly to brown. Before serving, heat the slices for a bit in the oven. This way you can wait until everyone is ready to eat.

Adult or Child: Preheat the oven to 325 degrees.

Child with Adult: Break the eggs into the mixing bowl. Whisk in the milk, heavy cream, sugar, salt, and vanilla. Add the challah slices. Let them soak for about 5 minutes, making sure you submerge the bread completely. You can use a plate to help you keep it down.

Adult with Child: Melt the butter in the frying pan over high heat, swirling it around to cover the bottom. Drain each piece of bread, then fry on both sides to get a golden brown color on the outside. Then transfer the pan to the oven for about 5 minutes and serve with maple syrup.

AUNT LORRAINE'S NOODLE KUGEL

Serves 8

INGREDIENTS

- ¼ cup (½ stick) unsalted butter or vegan spread
- 1 teaspoon vegetable oil
- 1 teaspoon salt
- 8 ounces dried broad egg noodles
- One 8-ounce package cream cheese
- ½ cup sugar
- 4 large eggs
- ¼ cup sour cream, plus more for serving
- ¼ cup cottage cheese
- 1 teaspoon ground cinnamon
- 1 teaspoon vanilla extract
- 2 cups milk
- 1 to 1½ cups sugarcoated Frosted Flakes
- Sour cream, for serving

EQUIPMENT

- 9-by-9-inch baking pan
- Large pot
- Colander
- Small saucepan
- Mixing bowls
- Sharp knife
- Fork or wire whisk
- Large wooden spoon
- Rubber spatula
- Small bowl

In Alsace-Lorraine and Germany, until the Middle Ages, Jews usually ate only one dish for a meal except on the Sabbath. A kugel became the Sabbath dessert, a sweet noodle or potato dish often made with dried fruit that sat right next to the long-cooking cholent in a public oven. A member of the family would bring the dish and often mark it with a symbol to identify it as theirs. When my children were little, I could cajole them into eating dishes they didn't want—as long as they knew a kugel was coming afterward.

For this recipe buy a box of Frosted Flakes cereal even though you know that your children shouldn't be eating so much sugar. But you don't make this dish every day, and that box can last you a lifetime of kugels unless your kids get to it for their morning cereal.

When I asked my children about their favorite kugel growing up, their answer was the kugel at monthly Shabbat dinners with friends. When I asked Diane Eichner, Aunt Lorraine's niece, for the recipe, she was delighted to share it. Now Diane is making it with her granddaughters, who love crushing the Frosted Flakes on top. Eight-year-old June has now moved onto the full prep. I have halved the recipe but otherwise it is a living testament to Aunt Lorraine.

Adult with child: Lightly grease the baking dish with some of the butter or vegan spread. Bring a large pot of salted water to a boil with the vegetable oil and salt (the oil helps to separate the strands). Cook the noodles according to the directions on the noodle package label, for about 5 minutes. Drain the pasta in a colander, and spread the noodles out in the baking pan. (The children will really enjoy doing this!)

Adult: Cream the softened butter, cream cheese, and sugar in a bowl. Add the eggs, sour cream, cottage cheese, cinnamon, vanilla extract, and milk. Don't worry if the mixture seems to have too much liquid.

Child: Using a large spoon, spoon the mixture over the noodles in the baking pan and mix well to combine and submerge the noodles. Cover and refrigerate for a few hours or overnight.

Adult with Child: When ready to bake, heat the oven to 350 degrees and uncover the kugel. Bake from 40 to 50 minutes until the center is pretty well set, then remove the kugel from the oven.

Adult with Child: Crush handfuls of Frosted Flakes over the kugel, spreading the cereal evenly. Return to the oven and bake for 10 to 20 minutes, until the sugar on the Frosted Flakes caramelizes. (Put on the oven light so the kids can watch so that you don't burn the top!) Cut into squares and serve directly from the oven or at room temperature with sour cream in a small bowl on the side.

Makes 4 shakes

INGREDIENTS

2 whole bananas, fresh or frozen

4 medjool dates, pitted, and chopped a bit if too big

¼ cup tahini

1 to 2 cups ice cubes

1½ cups unsweetened almond or regular milk

¼ teaspoon plus 4 pinches of ground cinnamon

EQUIPMENT

Knife

Blender

4 glasses

DATE TAHINI BANANA MILKSHAKE

To show how the times change, when I first went to Palm Springs, in the early 2000s, I discovered a date shake, something I hadn't ever tasted on the East Coast. Of course, I knew shakes but not date shakes. Today there is every kind of sweet and savory shake for breakfast and throughout the day. Clio, my editor Lexy's daughter, is a huge fan of date, tahina, and banana shakes, as are my grandchildren.

This is a great milk drink for Shavuot or a healthy vegan snack at any time of the year. It is also a wonderful way to use up the overripe bananas; peel them, then throw them in the freezer.

Child with Adult: Cut the bananas in four pieces, and throw them into the blender with the dates (making sure to remove the pits), tahini, 1 cup of the ice cubes, the almond or regular milk, and the ¼ teaspoon of cinnamon. Turn the blender on, and purée until the shake is smooth and creamy. Add more ice if you want it less creamy.

Child: Pour the shake into four glasses and top each with a pinch of additional cinnamon.

Note: When the banana peels start to brown, I peel the bananas and throw them into containers in the freezer, so I always have them ready for shakes, pancakes (page 106), or banana bread.

WATERMELON, CORN, CUCUMBER, AND FETA SALAD

Serves 6 to 8

INGREDIENTS

1 small watermelon

1 cup cooked corn

1 large cucumber

About 1 cup torn romaine lettuce

Juice of 1 lemon

3 tablespoons extra-virgin olive oil

1 clove garlic, peeled (optional)

Salt and freshly ground pepper, to taste

About 3 tablespoons chopped fresh mint

One 4-ounce block feta, torn into ½-inch pieces

EQUIPMENT

1 large sharp knife

1 cutting board

1 melon baller

1 large serving bowl

Jar

Microplane

My grandchildren love this salad, and it is a great opportunity for them to practice their cutting skills. My friend Cathy Sulzberger taught me the simplicity of using the microplane to grate garlic for the dressing. If your children don't like garlic, omit it.

Adult with Child: Cut the watermelon in half with a sharp knife and scoop out the watermelon with a melon baller to make about 3 cups. Put into a large serving bowl. Sprinkle in the corn. Either peel the cucumber or don't bother, cut it into ½-inch dice, and toss it in, and then add the torn-up romaine lettuce. Refrigerate the mixture for a few hours, until you're ready to serve.

Child with Adult: Squeeze the lemon juice into the olive oil in a small bowl. Microplane the garlic, if using, and sprinkle it into the dressing, along with salt and pepper. Refrigerate this dressing.

Child: Just before serving, remove the watermelon bowl from the fridge, pour the dressing over the salad, and sprinkle with the mint and broken-up pieces of feta.

APRICOT FRUIT LEATHERS

Makes about 4

INGREDIENTS

1 cup dried apricots

Hot water to cover

EQUIPMENT

Measuring cup

Mixing bowl

Strainer

Mortar and pestle, or food processor

Plastic wrap or wax paper

Rolling pin

We may think that fruit leathers were invented in America. Wrong! Even in Biblical times, before refined sugar, children had a sweet tooth. They snacked on fruit leathers and date jam before anyone knew what a cookie sweetened with sugar and puffed up with baking powder was. Who knows, maybe this is the oldest snack food known to mankind!

Child: Place the apricots in the water to cover, and let them soften. This will take about 15 minutes.

Adult with Child: Drain the apricots in a strainer, and put them into a mortar and pestle or food processor; the mortar and pestle are great fun for children to use to mash up the apricots. Once the fruit has been pulverized, place the leathers between two pieces of wax paper or plastic wrap. Roll them out as thinly as possible with a rolling pin, and leave them to dry for about 2 days in the wrap. Remove the wrap, roll up the leathers, and, using scissors, cut them into 3-inch widths. Nosh for a snack.

ACKNOWLEDGMENTS

Writing a cookbook, especially one for children, is tricky, and as always involves the help of many people. The following people gave me ideas and shared their recipes with me for the book: Diane Eichner, Rob Eshman, Mark Furstenberg, Valerie Gordon, Neil and Lianne Gottheimer, Chef Wojtek Gurtiakow, Tara Lazar, Rabbi Steve Leder, Ivy Lehmann, Ori Menashe, Cecile Mouthan, Yotam Ottolenghi, Marsha Pinson, Nancy Silverton, Audrey Singer, Mike Solomonov, and Cathy Sulzberger.

Once again, Gabriela Herman worked her magic with the photography and Rachael Fox, Grace Kennedy, Sarah Waldman, and Zoe Weitzman were a great team in assisting us. As my daughter Daniela marveled, "How did you pull it off, making my five-and-a-half-year-old children cooperate!" Kara Elder helped me once again with the updating and editing of the manuscript, and Hannah Wolfman-Arent and Amy Bartscherer helped with the testing. I want to thank the Weitzman National Museum of American Jewish History for graciously sharing some of their Judaica for the photographs, and Adas Israel Congregation's Gan HaYeled's teachers, who helped with the original book in 1987 and then again in 1995, and now with retired teacher Marsha Pinson helping me with so many ideas. Biblical quotations come from the Jewish Publication Society's 2017 edition of *Tanakh, the Holy Scriptures: The New JPS Translation According to the Traditional Hebrew Text.*

Lexy Bloom, my brilliant editor and the head of Knopf Cooks, had the good sense to listen to her eight-year-old daughter, Clio, who had such great ideas for this book—which I believe will be the first children's book for Knopf Cooks. The team at Knopf always amazes me—Sara Eagle, Kathleen Fridella, Morgan Hamilton, Kathy Hourigan, Altie Karper, Sarah New, Tom Pold, Casey Hampton, and Lisa Montebello—and I feel so privileged to be part of their publishing family. And, as always, my agent, David Black, is there for me whenever I need him.

Again, I want to thank my children Daniela, David, and Merissa, who had the patience to share their recollections of childhood foods and holidays with me. I also want to thank my daughters-in-law, Liv and Talia, who came to the Gerson game as adults. But most of all, I want to thank Daniela and Talia's six-year-old twins, Alma and Aviv, who have been making challah, muffins, and pomegranate punch, as well as emptying the dishwasher and putting things away, since they were two years old. It is they who have regenerated my heart with love for them and have sparked an interest for me in making this book come to life for yet another generation.

INDEX

(Page references in *italics* refer to illustrations.)

A

Adam and Eve, 130, 134
Aleichem, Sholem, 105, 122
Alma's Strawberry Pancakes, 106
almond(s):
  Caramel Chocolate Matzo Brittle, 170–1
  Chocolate Passover Cake, *172, 173,* 173–4
  Grandma's Seven Species Granola, 91–2, *93*
  symbolic meaning of, 130
Ambitious Kitchen website, 137
Antiochus, King, 105
apple(s), 49
  Cake Eden, 60, *61*
  and Cream Cheese Spread, 188
  Golden Harvest Tzimmes, 90
  Honey Cupcakes, 73
  Latkes, 110, *111*
  symbolic meaning of, 129–30
  Tree of Life Fruitful Salad, 134
  Vegetable Kugelettes, *164,* 165
Applesauce, 108
apricot(s):
  Chicken Tagine, Moroccan, *51,* 51–2, *53*
  Fruit Leathers, 198
  symbolic meaning of, 130
Aunt Lisl's Butter Cookies, 120, *121*
Aunt Lorraine's Noodle Kugel, 192–3
Australian Carrot Dip, 50
Aviv's Banana Pancakes, 106
avocado, in Tree of Life Fruitful Salad, 134

B

Bagels, 186–7
banana:
  Date Tahini Milkshake, 194, *194, 195*
  Pancakes, Aviv's, 106
barley, pearl:
  Children's Cholent: A Veggie-Bean Stew, 88–9
  Grandma's Seven Species Granola, 91–2, *93*
basil:
  Crustless Quiche with Cherry Tomatoes, Cheese, and, 59
  Pasta with Pesto and Green Beans, 95–6, *97*
Bavel, Bestia, and Saffy, Los Angeles, 191
beans, in Children's Cholent: A Veggie-Bean Stew, 88–9
Beard, James, 99
beverages:
  Date Tahini Banana Milkshake, 194, *194, 195*
  Grape Juice, 17
  Greek Lemonade, 74, *75*
  Pomegranate Punch, Persian, 58, *58*
Biblical foods, 49, 91
  pomegranates, 56
  Tzatziki (Biblical Yogurt Dip), 132, *133*
Blintzes, Cheese, 190
breads:
  Bagels, 186–7
  Lekoach, 68
  Pita, 148–9
  Zucchini, *99,* 99–100
  see also Challah
breakfast and brunch:
  Apple and Cream Cheese Spread, 188
  Apple Latkes, 110, *111*
  Aviv's Banana or Alma's Strawberry Pancakes, 106

breakfast and brunch *(continued)*:
- Bagels, 186–7
- Cheese Blintzes, 190
- Cherry Oatmeal Cookie Bars, *136,* 137–8
- French Toast, Saffron's Easy, 191
- Grandma's Seven Species Granola, 91–2, *93*
- at kibbutzim, 146
- Matzo Brei, 169
- Shakshuka (Eggs in Tomato Sauce), 36, *37*
- Tree of Life Fruitful Salad, 134
- Zucchini Bread, *99,* 99–100

Brownies, East and West, 112–14
buckwheat flour, in West Coast Gluten-Free Brownies from Valerie Confections in Echo Park, Los Angeles, 114
Burekas, Cheese or Spinach, 34–5
butter:
- Cookies, Aunt Lisl's, 120, *121*
- Homemade, 182

butternut squash:
- Golden Harvest Tzimmes, 90
- Lentil, and Carrot Soup, 76–7
- Sweet Potatoes, and Chickpeas, Sort of Sephardic, 54–5

C

cakes:
- Apple, Eden, 60, *61*
- Chocolate Almond, Passover, *172, 173,* 173–4
- Lemon Yogurt Pound, 154

candlestick holders, 16
Caramel Almond Chocolate Matzo Brittle, 170–1
carob, 129, 130
carrot(s):
- Children's Cholent: A Veggie-Bean Stew, 88–9
- Dip, Australian, 50
- Golden Harvest Tzimmes, 90
- Lentil, and Squash Soup, 76–7
- Sukkot Stuffed Vegetables, *85,* 85–6, *87*
- Vegetable Kugelettes, *164,* 165

Challah, *18,* 18–22, 20–2
- French Toast, Saffron's Easy, 191
- Rainbow, 23, *23–5*
- round, for Rosh Hashanah, 49
- serving at Sabbath table, 11–12, 15
- for Tu B'Shevat, 131, *131*

chametz, 160–61
cheese:
- Blintzes, 190
- Burekas, 34–5
- Cream, and Apple Spread, 188
- cream, in Aunt Lorraine's Noodle Kugel, 192–3
- Crustless Quiche with Cherry Tomatoes, Basil, and, 59
- Curd, Homemade, 183–4, *183–5*
- Farfel and, Passover-Style, 168
- Feta, Watermelon, Corn, and Cucumber Salad, 196, *197*
- goat, in Eggplant Gratin, 98
- grated, in Matzo Pizza, 166, *167*
- Veggie Quiche, 94

Cherry Oatmeal Cookie Bars, *136,* 137–8
chicken:
- Apricot Tagine, Moroccan, *51,* 51–2, *53*
- *kapparah* tradition and, 69
- Kreplach, 71
- Schnitzel Tenders, 33, *33*
- Soup with Matzo Balls, 28, *29,* 30
- Yemenite High Holy Day Soup, 69–70

chickpea(s):
- Falafel, 145
- Hummus, 26, *27*
- Pancakes, Vegan, 109
- at Purim, 143–4
- Sweet Potatoes, and Squash, Sort of Sephardic, 54–5

Child, Julia, 98
Children's Cholent: A Veggie-Bean Stew, 88–9
chocolate:
- Almond Caramel Matzo Brittle, 170–1
- Almond Passover Cake, *172, 173,* 173–4
- Chip Cookies, Golda Meir's, 38, *39*
- Chip Kisses, 175
- chips, in Mandelbrot, *40, 41,* 41–2
- East and West Brownies, 112–14
- Edible Dreidel, 118, *119*

Cholent, Children's: A Veggie-Bean Stew, 88–9
Chopped Israeli Salad, 146
circles, symbolism of, 49
coconut:
- Grandma's Seven Species Granola, 91–2, *93*
- Mandelbrot, *40, 41,* 41–2

cookies:
- Butter, Aunt Lisl's, 120, *121*
- Cherry Oatmeal Bars, *136,* 137–8
- Chocolate Chip, Golda Meir's, 38, *39*
- Hamantashen, *150, 151,* 151–2
- Mandelbrot, *40, 41,* 41–2

corn:
- Flynn's Orzo, 147
- Sukkot Stuffed Vegetables, *85,* 85–6, *87*
- Watermelon, Cucumber, and Feta Salad, 196, *197*

cornmeal, in Aviv's Banana or Alma's Strawberry Pancakes, 106
crafts, for Sabbath table, 15–16
cream cheese:
- and Apple Spread, 188
- Aunt Lorraine's Noodle Kugel, 192–3

Crustless Quiche with Cherry Tomatoes, Basil, and Cheese, 59
cucumber:
- Chopped Israeli Salad, 146
- Tzatziki (Biblical Yogurt Dip), 132, *133*
- Watermelon, Corn, and Feta Salad, 196, *197*
- Yogurt-Salad, Persian, 189

cupcakes:
- Apple-Honey, 73
- Ice Cream, Edible Menorah, 115–16, *116, 117*

Curd Cheese, Homemade, 183–4, *183, 184, 185*

D

date(s), 49
Nut-Free Haroset, 162
Peanut Butter–Stuffed Figs and, 135
Tahini Banana Milkshake, 194, *194, 195*
Tree of Life Fruitful Salad, 134
desserts. *See* sweets
Deuteronomy, 4, 91
dips:
Carrot, Australian, 50
Hummus, 26, *27*
Tzatziki (Biblical Yogurt Dip), 132, *133*
Dreidel, Edible, 118, *119*
Dumplings, Mushroom Kreplach, 72

E

East and West Brownies, 112–14
Edible Dreidel, 118, *119*
eggplant:
Children's Cholent: A Veggie-Bean Stew, 88–9
Gratin, 98
eggs:
Aunt Lorraine's Noodle Kugel, 192–3
Crustless Quiche with Cherry Tomatoes, Basil, and Cheese, 59
Farfel and Cheese, Passover-Style, 168
French Toast, Saffron's Easy, 191
Matzo Brei, 169
in Tomato Sauce (Shakshuka), 36, *37*
Veggie Quiche, 94
Eichner, Diane, 192
Esther, Queen, 143, 144, 153
etrog (fragrant yellow fruit of citron), 84
Exodus, 105, 159

F

Falafel, 145
Farfel and Cheese, Passover-Style, 168
Feinberg family, Cincinnati, 165
Feta, Watermelon, Corn, and Cucumber Salad, 196, *197*
Figs, Peanut Butter–Stuffed Dates and, 135
filo dough, in Cheese or Spinach Burekas, 34–5
Flynn's Orzo, 147
French Toast, Saffron's Easy, 191
From Baghdad to Bombay (Sofaer), 17
Fruitful Salad, Tree of Life, 134
fruit(s):
Leathers, Apricot, 198
symbolic meanings of, 129–30
see also specific fruits

G

Gerson, Allan, x, 11, 12–14, 41, 105
Gluten-Free West Coast Brownies from Valerie Confections in Echo Park, Los Angeles, 114
goat cheese, in Eggplant Gratin, 98
Golda Meir's Chocolate Chip Cookies, 38, *39*
Golden Harvest Tzimmes, 90
Goldman, Marcy, 170
Grandma's Seven Species Granola, 91–2, *93*
Granola, Seven Species, Grandma's, 91–2, *93*
Grape Juice, 17
Gratin, Eggplant, 98
Greek cooking:
Lemonade, 74, *75*
Nut-Free Haroset, 162
Tzatziki (Biblical Yogurt Dip), 132, *133*
Green Beans, Pasta with Pesto and, 95–6, *97*
groggers, 143
Gurtiakow, Wojtek, 76

H

Haggadah, 159, 160
Halvah, 153
Haman, 143
Hamantashen, *150, 151,* 151–2
Hanukkah, 101–23
dreidel song and game for, 118
menorah for, 105, 115
menus for, 103
symbolism and observance of, 103
Haroset, Nut-Free, 162
Havdalah, 43, 84
Honey-Apple Cupcakes, 73
Hummus, 26, *27*

I

Ice Cream Cupcake Edible Menorah, 115–16, *116, 117*
Israeli cooking:
Chicken Schnitzel Tenders, 33, *33*
Chopped Salad, 146
Falafel, 145
Sufganiyot, 122–3
Sukkot Stuffed Vegetables, *85,* 85–6, *87*
Iza Pziza Dairy Visitor Center, Israel, 183

J

johnnycake meal, in Aviv's Banana or Alma's Strawberry Pancakes, 106

K

kapparah tradition, 69
kibbutzim, breakfast at, 146
kiddush cups, 12, 16
kidney beans, in Children's Cholent: A Veggie-Bean Stew, 88–9
Knishes, Quick, 31–2
kosher dietary laws, 3–5
Kreplach, 71
Mushroom, Dumplings, 72
Kugel, Noodle, Aunt Lorraine's, 192–3
Kugelettes, Vegetable, *164,* 165

L

latke(s):
Apple, 110, *111*
party menu, 103
Potato, 107
Lazar, Tara, 72
Lekoach, 68

Lemonade, Greek, 74, *75*
Lemon Yogurt Pound Cake, 154
Lentil, Squash, and Carrot Soup, 76–7
Leviticus, 3, 4, 148
Licht, Dottie, 190
life-cycle events, bagels in, 186
lima beans, in Children's Cholent: A Veggie-Bean Stew, 88–9
Lox Stock & Barrel, Bondi Beach, Australia, 50
lulav, 84, 161

M

Mandelbrot, *40, 41,* 41–2
marshmallows, in Edible Dreidel, 118, *119*
matzo:
- Balls, 30
- Brei, 169
- Brittle, Almond Caramel Chocolate Matzo, 170–1
- Farfel and Cheese, Passover-Style, 168
- meal, in Vegetable Kugelettes, *164,* 165
- Passover and, 159–60
- Pizza, 166, *167*

Menashe, Ori, 191
menorah:
- Ice Cream Cupcake Edible, 115–16, *116, 117*
- symbolism of, 105, 115

Michael Cohen's (restaurant), Jerusalem, 85
Milkshake, Date Tahini Banana, 194, *194, 195*
mint, in Tzatziki (Biblical Yogurt Dip), 132, *133*
Mordecai, 143
Moroccan Apricot Chicken Tagine, *51,* 51–2, *53*
Mozza, Los Angeles, 95
mushroom(s):
- Kreplach, 71
- Kreplach Dumplings, 72

N

Noodle Kugel, Aunt Lorraine's, 192–3
Nut-Free Haroset, 162
nuts:
- symbolic meanings of, 129–30
- *see also* almond(s); pecans; walnuts

O

oat(meal)(s):
- Cherry Cookie Bars, *136,* 137–8
- Grandma's Seven Species Granola, 91–2, *93*

orange, in Tree of Life Fruitful Salad, 134
orzo:
- Flynn's, 147
- Sukkot Stuffed Vegetables, *85,* 85–6, *87*

Ottolenghi, Yotam, 147

P

pancakes:
- Apple Latkes, 110, *111*
- Aviv's Banana or Alma's Strawberry, 106
- Chickpea, Vegan, 109
- Potato Latkes, 107

Passover, 155–75
- menus for, 157
- symbolism and observance of, 159–61

Passover Chocolate Almond Cake, *172, 173,* 173–4
Passover-Style Farfel and Cheese, 168
pasta:
- Orzo, Flynn's, 147
- orzo, in Sukkot Stuffed Vegetables, *85,* 85–6, *87*
- with Pesto and Green Beans, 95–6, *97*

Peanut Butter–Stuffed Figs and Dates, 135
peas, in Sukkot Stuffed Vegetables, *85,* 85–6, *87*
pecans:
- Chocolate Chip Kisses, 175
- Tree of Life Fruitful Salad, 134

peppers:
- Chopped Israeli Salad, 146
- Sukkot Stuffed Vegetables, *85,* 85–6, *87*

Persian cooking:
- Halvah, 153
- Pomegranate Punch, 58, *58*

Pesto, Pasta with Green Beans and, 95–6, *97*
pistachios, in Halvah, 153
Pita Bread, 148–9
Pizza, Matzo, 166, *167*
place mats, 15
pomegranate(s), 49, 56, 68
- Grandma's Seven Species Granola, 91–2, *93*
- peeling, 57
- Punch, Persian, 58, *58*
- symbolic meaning of, 130
- Tree of Life Fruitful Salad, 134

potato(es):
- Children's Cholent: A Veggie-Bean Stew, 88–9
- Knishes, Quick, 31–2
- Latkes, 107

Pound Cake, Lemon Yogurt, 154
Psalms, 181
Purim, 71, 139–54
- menus for, 141
- symbolism and observance of, 143–4

Q

quiches:
- Crustless, with Cherry Tomatoes, Basil, and Cheese, 59
- Veggie, 94

R

Rainbow Challah, 23, *23–5*
rice, in Sukkot Stuffed Vegetables, *85,* 85–6, *87*
Rosh Hashanah, 45–60
- menus for, 47
- symbolism and observance of, 49, 54

S

Sabbath, or Shabbat, 7–43
- cholent and, 88
- crafts for use on, 15–16
- Havdalah and, 43, 84
- menus for, 9, 45, 81, 103
- symbolism and observance of, 11–14

Saffron's Easy French Toast, 191
salads:
- Chopped Israeli, 146
- Cucumber Yogurt, Persian, 189
- Tree of Life Fruitful, 134
- Watermelon, Corn, Cucumber, and Feta, 196, *197*

Seder, 159–61
- special plates and cups for, 160

Seder Salad, A, 163
Sephardic traditions:
- Sort of Sephardic Sweet Potatoes, Chickpeas, and Squash, 54–5
- Tu B'Shevat Seder, 130, 135

Seven Species Granola, Grandma's, 91–2, *93*
Shakshuka (Eggs in Tomato Sauce), 36, *37*
shalach manot plate, 141
- Aunt Lisl's Butter Cookies, 120, *121*
- Chocolate Chip Kisses, 175
- Golda Meir's Chocolate Chip Cookies, 38, *39*
- Hamantashen, *150, 151,* 151–2
- Lemon Yogurt Pound Cake, 154
- Peanut Butter-Stuffed Figs and Dates, 135

Shavuot, 177–98
- menus for, 179
- symbolism and observance of, 181

Silverton, Nancy, 95
Simchat Torah, 71
Singer, Audrey, 137
Sofaer, Pearl, 17
Solomonov, Mike, 173
Sort of Sephardic Sweet Potatoes, Chickpeas, and Squash, 54–5
soups:
- Chicken, with Matzo Balls, 28, *29,* 30
- Lentil, Squash, and Carrot, 76–7
- Yemenite High Holy Day, 69–70

Spinach Burekas, 34–5
squash:
- butternut, in Golden Harvest Tzimmes, 90
- Lentil, and Carrot Soup, 76–7
- Sweet Potatoes, and Chickpeas, Sort of Sephardic, 54–5

strawberry(ies):
- Edible Dreidel, 118, *119*
- Pancakes, Alma's, 106

Stuffed Vegetables, Sukkot, *85,* 85–6, *87*
Sufganiyot, 122–3
sukkah, 83–4, 88
Sukkot, 79–100, 161
- menus for, 81
- symbolism and observance of, 83–4

Sulzberger, Cathy, 194
sweet potato(es):
- Chickpeas, and Squash, Sort of Sephardic, 54–5
- Children's Cholent: A Veggie-Bean Stew, 88–9
- Golden Harvest Tzimmes, 90
- Vegetable Kugelettes, *164,* 165

sweets:
- Almond Caramel Chocolate Matzo Brittle, 170–1
- Apple Cake Eden, 60, *61*
- Apple-Honey Cupcakes, 73
- Apricot Fruit Leathers, 198
- Butter Cookies, Aunt Lisl's, 120, *121*
- Cherry Oatmeal Cookie Bars, *136,* 137–8
- Chocolate Chip Cookies, Golda Meir's, 38, *39*
- Chocolate Chip Kisses, 175
- East and West Brownies, 112–14
- Halvah, 153
- Hamantashen, *150, 151,* 151–2
- Ice Cream Cupcake Edible Menorah, 115–16, *116, 117*
- Lemon Yogurt Pound Cake, 154
- Noodle Kugel, Aunt Lorraine's, 192–3
- Nut-Free Haroset, 162
- Passover Chocolate Almond Cake, *172, 173,* 173–4
- Peanut Butter-Stuffed Figs and Dates, 135
- Sufganiyot, 122–3
- Vegetable Kugelettes, *164,* 165

symbolic meanings of fruits and nuts, 129–30

T

Tagine, Apricot Chicken, Moroccan, *51,* 51–2, *53*
tahini:
- Date Banana Milkshake, 194, *194, 195*
- Halvah, 153

Talisman, Mark and Jessica, 186
Temple, Jerusalem, 4, 18, 105, 109, 160, 181
tomato(es):
- Cherry, Crustless Quiche with Basil, Cheese, and, 59
- Chopped Israeli Salad, 146
- Flynn's Orzo, 147
- Sauce, Eggs in (Shakshuka), 36, *37*
- sauce, in Matzo Pizza, 166, *167*

Torah portion of the week, 14
Treasury of Jewish Holiday Baking, A (Goldman), 170
Tree of Life Fruitful Salad, 134
tree planting in Israel, 130
Tu B'Shevat, 125–37
- menus, 127
- symbolism and observance of, 129–30

Tu B'Shevat Challah, 131, *131*
Tzatziki (Biblical Yogurt Dip), 132, *133*
Tzimmes, Golden Harvest, 90

V

Valerie Confections, Echo Park, Los Angeles, 114
Vegan Chickpea Pancakes, 109
vegetable(s):
  Children's Cholent: A Veggie-Bean Stew, 88–9
  Eggplant Gratin, 98
  Golden Harvest Tzimmes, 90
  Kugelettes, *164,* 165
  A Seder Salad, 163
  Stuffed, Sukkot, *85,* 85–6, *87*
  Sweet Potatoes, Chickpeas, and Squash, Sort of Sephardic, 54–5
Veggie Quiche, 94
Vongerichten, Jean-Georges, 173

W

walnuts:
  Chocolate Chip Kisses, 175
  Halvah, 153
Watermelon, Corn, Cucumber, and Feta Salad, 196, *197*
West Coast Gluten-Free Brownies from Valerie Confections in Echo Park, Los Angeles, 114
wheat berries, in Grandma's Seven Species Granola, 91–2, *93*

Y

Yemenite cooking:
  Dinner Before the Fast menu, 65
  High Holy Day Soup, 69–70
  Lekoach, 68
yogurt:
  Cucumber Salad, Persian, 189
  frozen, in Cupcake Edible Menorah, 115–16, *116, 117*
  Lemon Pound Cake, 154
  Tzatziki (Biblical Yogurt Dip), 132, *133*
Yom Kippur, 63–76
  breaking the fast of, 65, 67, 76
  menus for, 65

Z

Zahav Restaurant, Philadelphia, 173
zucchini:
  Bread, *99,* 99–100
  Children's Cholent: A Veggie-Bean Stew, 88–9

A NOTE ON THE TYPE

This book was set in Legacy Serif. Ronald Arnholm (b. 1939) designed the Legacy family after being inspired by the 1470 edition of *Eusebius* set in the roman type of Nicolas Jenson. This revival type maintains much of the character of the original. Its serifs, stroke weights, and varying curves give Legacy Serif its distinct appearance. It was released by the International Typeface Corporation in 1992.

Composed by North Market Street Graphics
Lancaster, Pennsylvania

Printed and bound by C&C Offset, China

Designed by Casey Hampton